Give Me Five!

PUPIL'S BOOK 2

My name is ______________________.

macmillan education

Joanne Ramsden • Donna Shaw

Course consultants: Rocío Gutiérrez Burgos and Mónica Pérez Is

Syllabus

S Let's go back to school!	Level 1 vocabulary School subjects The alphabet	*What's his / her name?* *His / Her name is Jake / Molly.*

	Vocabulary	Grammar	Phonics
1 Move your body	Sports Actions	*I play (tennis). I go (rollerblading).* *Do you (go skateboarding)? Yes, I do. No, I don't.* *He (throws) the ball. She (catches) the ball.*	Alternative vowel spellings **ai – ay**: sn**ai**ls pl**ay** r**ai**n d**ay**
2 Let's go shopping!	Food Numbers 10–50	*Can I have (a yoghurt / an apple / some potatoes), please?* *How much is this (lemon)?* *How much are these (carrots)?*	Alternative vowel spellings **ee – ea**: qu**ee**n J**ea**n **ea**ts m**ea**t gr**ee**n sh**ee**p ch**ee**se
3 At the zoo	Wild animals Animal body parts	*It's got (long hair). Has it got (long hair)? Yes, it has. No, it hasn't.* *Have they got (four legs)? Yes, they have. No, they haven't.* *It hasn't got (a beak). They haven't got (wings).*	Alternative vowel spellings **oo – ui**: kangar**oo** g**oo**se swims**ui**t fr**ui**t j**ui**ce p**oo**l
My project 1: Pets	Pets	*Have you got any pets?* *Yes, I have. I've got (two dogs and a turtle). No, I haven't.*	*Its name is (Ben).* *It lives in (my house).*
4 The nature trail	On a nature trail Prepositions of movement	*What are you doing? I'm (climbing).* *Are you (swimming)? Yes, I am. No, I'm not.* *What's he / she doing? He's / She's (running up a hill).*	Alternative vowel spellings **or – al**: h**or**se sh**or**ts w**al**ks t**al**ks st**or**m
5 The frozen lake	Actions Adjectives	*What are you doing? We're (skating).* *Are you (dancing)? Yes, we are. No, we aren't.* *Are they (playing)? Yes, they are. No, they aren't.* *He's got a (dirty) hat.*	Alternative vowel spellings **ow – oa**: sn**ow**man g**oa**t c**oa**t r**ow** yell**ow** b**oa**t rainb**ow**
6 All year round	Seasonal activities Ordinal numbers	*What do you / they do (in autumn)?* *We (go to the beach). They (open presents).* *Do they (celebrate Halloween)? Yes, they do. No, they don't. When's your birthday? My birthday is on the (tenth of June).*	Alternative vowel spellings **ur – ir**: p**ur**ple t**ur**tle b**ir**thday f**ir**st th**ir**d
My project 2: Jobs	Jobs	*A doctor helps people.* *A firefighter puts out fires.*	*He's / She's (a vet).* *He / She (helps animals).*
7 My house	Rooms in the house Objects	*There's / There isn't a (garage).* *There are / There aren't any (bedrooms).* *Whose is this (watch)? It's mine / yours / his / hers.*	Alternative vowel spellings **ow – ou**: br**ow**n c**ow** l**ou**d m**ou**se ar**ou**nd h**ou**se
8 All around the town	Places in a town Directions	*Is there a (bank)? Yes, there is. No, there isn't.* *Are there any (museums)? Yes, there are. No, there aren't.* *How do I get to the (post office)? Turn (left). / Go straight on.*	Alternative vowel spellings **y – igh**: fl**y** l**igh**t n**igh**t
9 Holiday fun	Holiday places Irregular plural nouns	*Where were you yesterday? I was at the (circus).* *Who's that (man)? He's my (uncle).* *Who are those (children)? They're my (cousins).*	Alternative vowel spellings **ear – air**: b**ear** p**ear** st**air**s funf**air**
My project 3: Time	Time	*What time is it?* *It's (eight o'clock).*	*What time do you (get up)? I (get up) at (a quarter past eight).*
Festivals	Harvest Festival	Carnival	

What's your favourite subject?
My favourite subject is (English).

How do you spell (English)?

Literacy	Culture	21st Century Skills	Cross-curricular links
A poem	Sports Day	21st **Ways of working:** joining in	**Science:** Joints; Muscles; Safety equipment for sports **Arts and Crafts:** Lines and shapes
A recipe	Pancake Day	21st **Digital skills:** finding recipes online	**Science:** Health, growth and energy; Balanced meals **Arts and Crafts:** Natural shapes
Fact files	Garden wildlife	21st **Ways of thinking:** sorting information	**Science:** Vertebrate and invertebrate animals; What animals eat **Arts and Crafts:** Primary and secondary colours
Pets class book			**Science:** Classifying animals; How animals are born **Arts and Crafts:** Lines, shapes and colours
An adventure story	Forest schools	21st **Living in the world:** looking after the environment	**Science:** Plants; Trees, bushes and grass; Parts of a tree; Evergreen and deciduous trees **Arts and Crafts:** Shapes and colours in nature
A fable	Winter activities	21st **Ways of thinking:** being creative	**Science:** Types of land **Arts and Crafts:** Different materials
A traditional rhyme	Seasonal festivals	21st **Ways of working:** doing a survey	**Science:** The seasons and the Sun **Arts and Crafts:** Patterns, lines, spaces and colours
Class jobs wall display			**Science:** Where people work; People who help us **Arts and Crafts:** Art in the city
A play script	Bedrooms	21st **Living in the world:** helping at home	**Science:** Types of materials; Properties of materials; Natural and manufactured materials **Arts and Crafts:** Pottery
An invitation	The emergency services	21st **Living in the world:** crossing the road safely	**Science:** Using maps **Arts and Crafts:** Movement
A diary	Summer holidays	21st **Digital skills:** using a digital camera	**Science:** Machines **Arts and Crafts:** Warm and cool colours
Daily routines			**Science:** Clocks in the past; Measuring time; Timelines **Arts and Crafts:** Photography

Cambridge Exams Practice Practice for the YLE Pre A1 Starters Exam (see p119 for syllabus)

Starter Unit

Let's go back to school!

Lesson 1

1 **Find and say.**

five animals five toys five classroom objects
five places five clothes five things to eat five shapes

2 **Find and say the numbers.**

3 **Listen and point. Sing *We've got our school bags*.** CD1 1

We've got our school bags.
We're ready for school.
We're on our way.
Let's go!

We're ready to listen.
We're ready to sing.
We're ready to speak English.

Chorus

We're ready to read.
We're ready to write.
We're ready to speak English.

Chorus

4 **Listen and act out.** CD1 3

Key learning outcomes: identify and say vocabulary from Level 1
Language: *What's his / her name? His / Her name is (Jake / Molly).*

1 Listen and point. CD1 4
Say *The school subjects* chant.

2 Listen and repeat. Act out. CD1 5

3 Listen and point. CD1 6

Key learning outcomes: identify and say eight school subjects
Language: *What's your favourite subject? My favourite subject is (English).*

S Lesson 3

1 **Listen and point. Say the alphabet.** CD1 7

2 **Listen and sing *The alphabet*.** CD1 8

3 **Talk Partners Listen and read. Ask and answer.** CD1 9

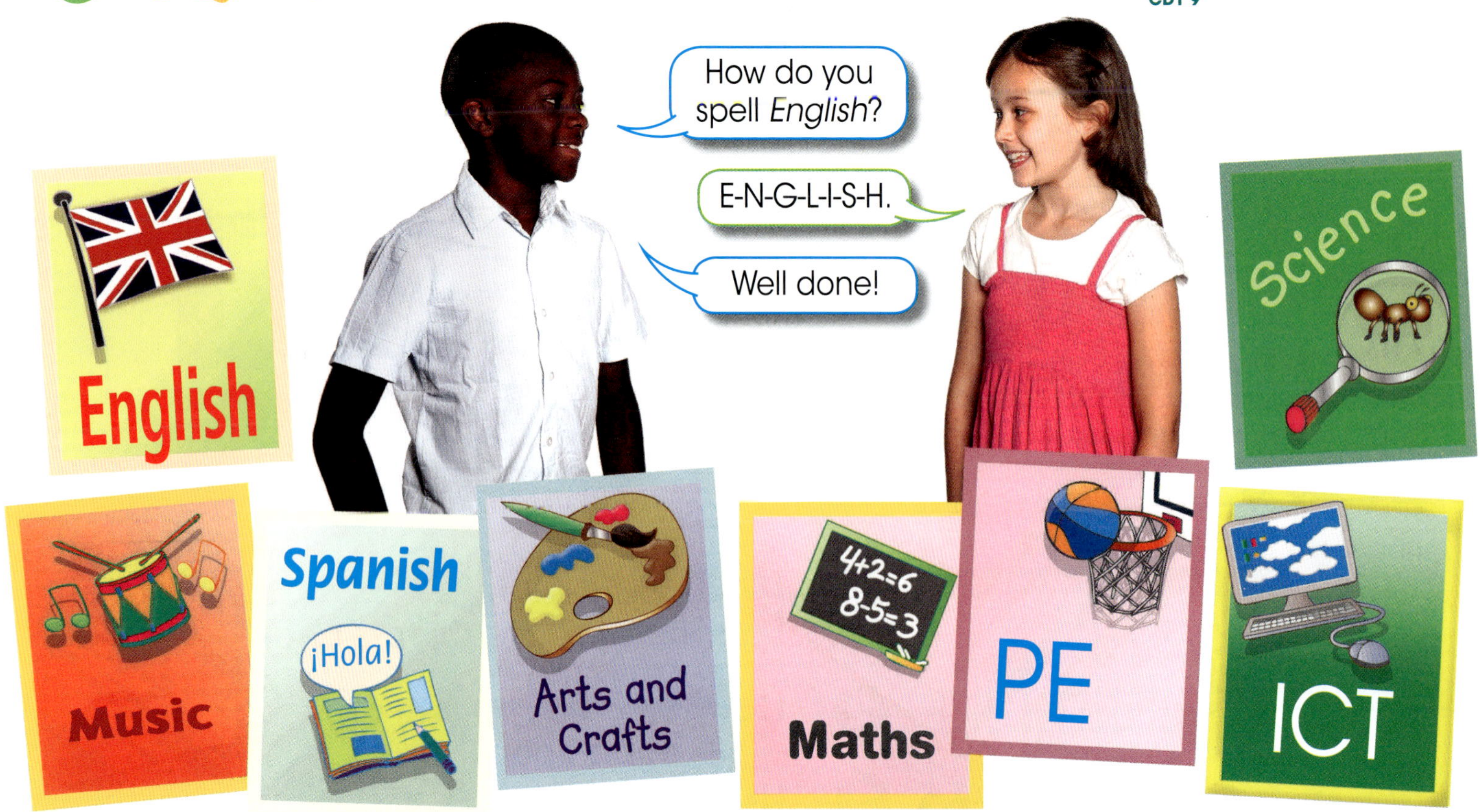

Key learning outcomes: sing the alphabet song and spell out words
Language: *How do you spell (English)?*

1 Listen and read. Act out. CD1 11

The storm

Now watch the animated story!

Key learning outcomes: read, listen and understand a story about the magic bike and a storm

Language: *It's (cloudy) today. Is it (raining)? Yes, it is.*

Unit 1 Move your body

1 **Listen and point. Sing *Do you play any sports?*** CD1 12

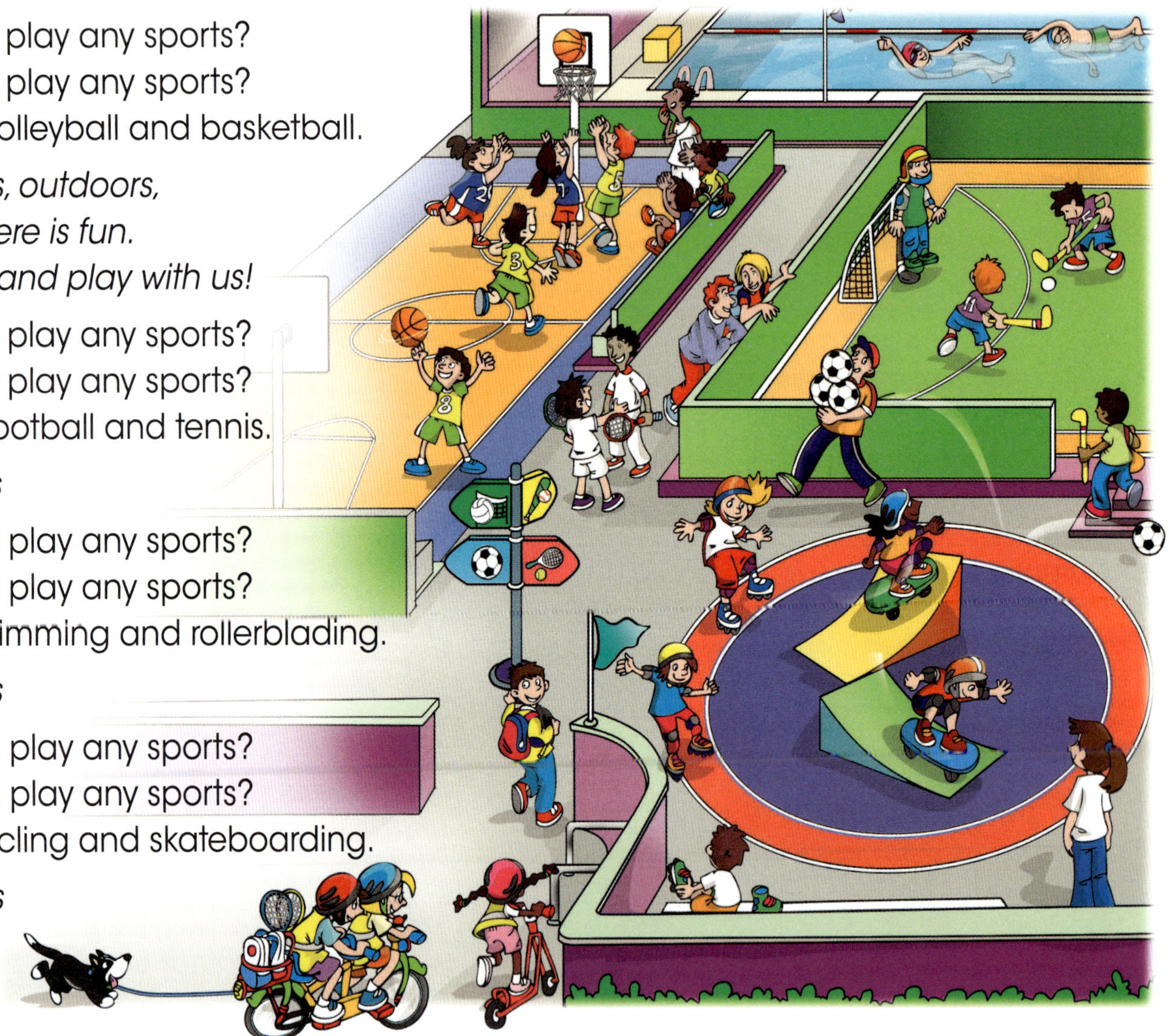

Do you play any sports?
Do you play any sports?
I play volleyball and basketball.

Indoors, outdoors,
anywhere is fun.
Come and play with us!

Do you play any sports?
Do you play any sports?
I play football and tennis.

Chorus

Do you play any sports?
Do you play any sports?
I go swimming and rollerblading.

Chorus

Do you play any sports?
Do you play any sports?
I go cycling and skateboarding.

Chorus

2 **Read and stick the ten stickers. Listen and say the chant.** CD1 14

football basketball tennis baseball skateboarding

Learning to learn → **Spelling: go to page 15 in your Activity Book.**

Key learning outcomes: identify and say ten sports; sing a song about sports
Vocabulary: sports

1 Listen and repeat. Act out.

CD1 15

Grammar

I go rollerblading.

Do you play tennis?

Yes, I do. No, I don't.

2 Listen and tick (✓).

CD1 16

1

2

3

cycling volleyball rollerblading hockey swimming

Key learning outcomes: use present simple: 'I' and 'you'

Grammar: *I go rollerblading. Do you (play tennis)? Yes, I do. No, I don't.*

Before you read

What sports are in the story?

1 Listen and read. Act out. CD1 17

The very busy week

1 Molly loves sport. Every day, she goes to the sports centre. Every day, she plays a different sport.

2 Today is Monday. Molly plays tennis on Monday.

3 Today is Tuesday. Molly plays football on Tuesday.

4 Today is Wednesday. Molly plays basketball on Wednesday.

Key learning outcomes: read, listen and understand a story about Molly's activities
Language: *I play baseball. Molly plays tennis on Monday.*

Now watch the animated story!

After you read

➔ Go to page 8 in your Activity Book.

2 **Values** Read and write.

throw away organise play

Remember to ________________ your things.

1 Listen, point and say.

CD1 18

hit

jump

kick

bounce

throw

catch

2 Listen and point. Sing *He's a superstar!*

CD1 19

Jump! Kick! Hit the ball!
Throw! Catch! Bounce the ball!

He's a superstar!
He runs like the wind.
He runs and he jumps
And he kicks the ball.
He's a superstar!

Chorus

She's a superstar!
She runs like the wind.
She throws and she catches
And she bounces the ball.
She's a superstar!

Chorus

3 Talk Partners Listen and repeat. Play a game.

CD1 20

Key learning outcomes: describe and guess a sport
Vocabulary: actions **Grammar:** *He (throws) the ball. She (catches) the ball.*

1 Listen and say. CD1 22

ai – ay – ai – ay. Snails play in the rain all day.

2 Listen and match. CD1 23

Monday Tuesday Wednesday Thursday Friday Saturday Sunday

3 Talk Partners Make and play the game.

Teacher's Resource Bank: Unit 1

Key learning outcomes: play a communication game about sports
Phonics: 'ai' and 'ay' spellings

1 Listen and read. Answer.

CD1 24

1 This is the egg and spoon race. We put an egg on a spoon and we run to the finish line.

2 This is the sack race. We get in a sack and we jump very fast.

3 This is the wheelbarrow race. My friend holds my legs and I walk on my hands.

4 This is the balloon toss. We throw and catch balloons. Be careful! The balloons contain water.

Think about your culture

What sports do you play at school?

Key learning outcomes: read about Sports Day in Britain; think about the sports you play at school

Text type: **A poem**

Before you read

1 Which balls do you think are in the poem? Circle.

2 Listen and read the poem. CD1 26

After you read

➔ Go to page 12 in your Activity Book.

1 Listen and number. Write and say. CD1 27

______ ______ ______

1 

______ ______ football ______

______ ______ ______

2 Talk Partners Listen. Look at Activity 1. Ask and answer. CD1 28

Do you play tennis?

Yes, I do.

Do you go skateboarding?

No, I don't.

3 Cooperative learning Sing *Well done!* CD1 29

Key learning outcomes: review language in the unit
Language: sports and *Do you …?*

Welcome back to Channel 21! Today's programme is about Sports Day. What sports do you play at school?

1 **Watch the video. Number the pictures.**

2 **Watch the video again. Read and tick (✓) or cross (✗).**

1 The girls win the tug of war. ✗

2 The boys can't skip. ☐

3 The eggs are all different colours. ☐

4 All the children join in. ☐

3 **Read and circle.**

Joining in

It's important to join in with the activities on Sports Day. What games do you like?

1 I (***like***) / ***don't like*** the egg and spoon race.

2 I ***like*** / ***don't like*** the tug of war.

3 I ***like*** / ***don't like*** the sack race

4 I ***like*** / ***don't like*** the three-legged race.

Key learning outcomes: watch and understand a video about sports day

21st **Ways of working:** learn to join in

Unit 2

Let's go shopping!

1 **Listen and point. Sing *Let's go shopping!*** CD1 31

Let's go shopping
And buy some food!

Bread and meat.
Put them in the bag!

Yoghurt and peaches,
Bread and meat.
Put them in the bag!

Green beans and carrots,
Yoghurt and peaches,
Bread and meat.
Put them in the bag!

Tomatoes and potatoes,
Green beans and carrots,
Yoghurt and peaches,
Bread and meat.
Put them in the bag!

Sweets and lemons,
Tomatoes and potatoes,
Green beans and carrots,
Yoghurt and peaches,
Bread and meat.
Put them in the bag!

Let's go shopping
And buy some food!

2 **Read and stick the ten stickers. Listen and say the chant.** CD1 33

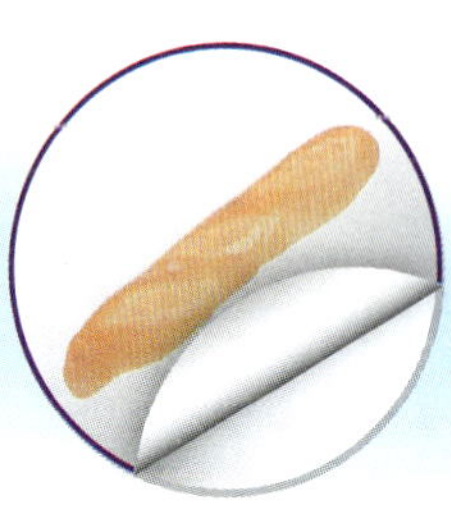

bread | pineapples | carrots | potatoes | green beans

Learning to learn → **Spelling: go to page 25 in your Activity Book.**

Key learning outcomes: identify and say ten food items; sing a song about shopping
Vocabulary: food

1 Listen and repeat. Act out. CD1 34

Grammar

a peach
an apple
some bread
some carrots

2 Listen and circle. CD1 35

1 

2 

3 

4 

tomatoes | yoghurt | sweets | peaches | lemons

Key learning outcomes: use indefinite articles: a / an / some
Grammar: *Can I have (a tomato / an apple / some sweets), please?*

Before you read Look at the pictures. What do Jake and Molly buy?

1 Listen and read. Act out. CD1 36

The naughty parrot

Key learning outcomes: read, listen and understand a story about a naughty parrot
Language: *Can I have some bread, please? How much are these (green beans)? They're (25 cents).*

5

6

7

8

Now watch the animated story!

After you read

2 **Values** **Read and write.**

thank you　　sorry　　please

It's important to say ______________ when you ask for something.

Values: saying please

2 Lesson 4 **Vocabulary and Grammar**

1 **Listen, point and say.** CD1 37

ten 10

twenty 20

thirty 30

forty 40

fifty 50

2 **Listen and point. Sing** ***How much is this?*** CD1 38

How much is this lemon?
Ten, twenty, thirty, forty, fifty cents.
It's ten cents.
Great! I'll take it.

How much is this bread?
Ten, twenty, thirty, forty, fifty cents.
It's twenty cents.
Great! I'll take it.

How much are these carrots?
Ten, twenty, thirty, forty, fifty cents.
They're thirty cents.
Great! I'll take them.

How much are these sweets?
Ten, twenty, thirty, forty, fifty cents.
They're forty cents.
Great! I'll take them.

3 **Talk Partners** **Listen and repeat. Act out.** CD1 39

How much are these?

They're thirty-six cents.

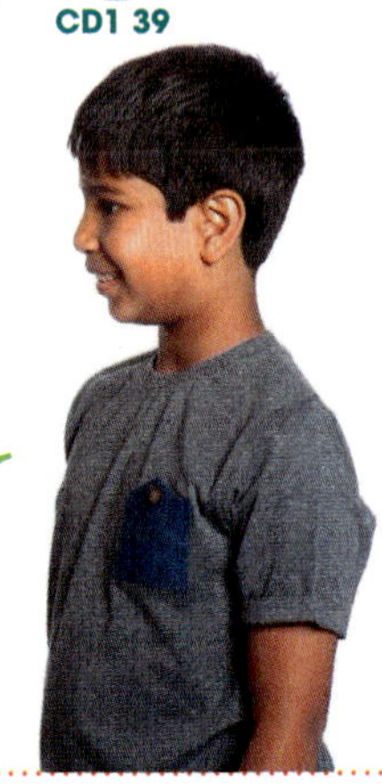

Key learning outcomes: ask and answer questions about the price of food
Vocabulary: numbers 10–50 **Grammar:** *How much is this (lemon)?*

1 Listen and say. CD1 41

2 Listen and write. CD1 42

1
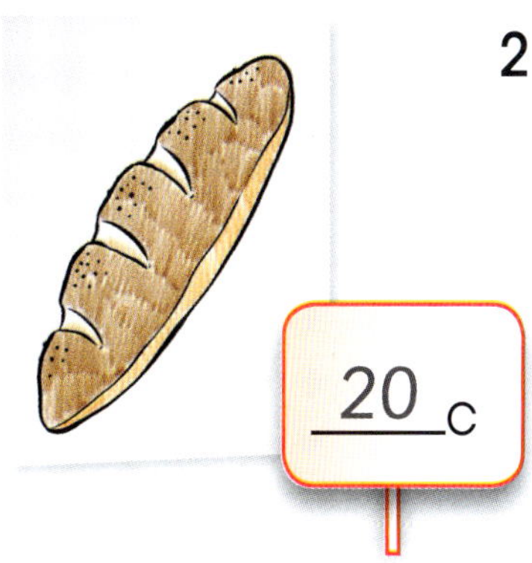

2
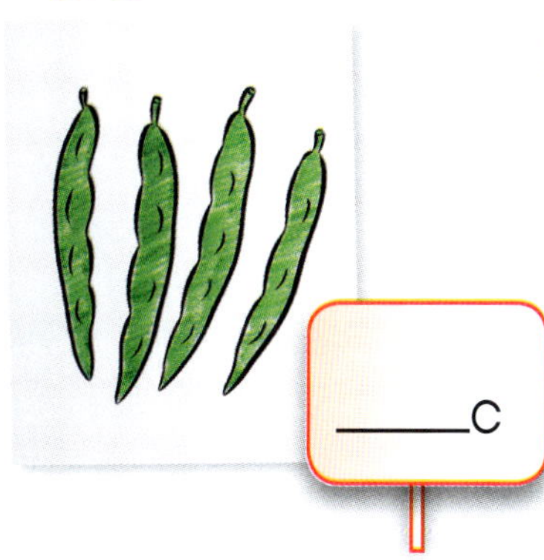

3

4
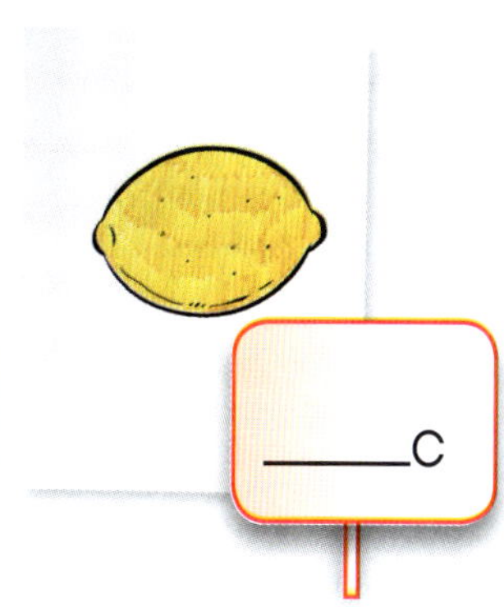

3 **Cooperative learning** Sing *What do I need to do?* CD1 43

4 **Talk Partners** Make and play the game.

Teacher's Resource Bank: Unit 2

Key learning outcomes: play a communication game about shopping
Phonics: 'ee' and 'ea' spellings

1 Listen and read. Answer.

CD1 44

In Britain, there's a special day called Pancake Day. We make pancakes and we have races with them!

1 We help Mum make the pancakes. We put flour, milk and two eggs in a bowl. Then, we mix it.

2 Mum cooks the pancakes. She tosses a pancake in the air. Then, she catches it again.

3 We eat our pancakes. I put chocolate on my pancake. My sister puts sugar and lemon on hers.

4 At school, we have pancake races. We run and toss the pancake at the same time. It's good fun!

Think about your culture

Do you have a special food day in your country?

Key learning outcomes: read about Pancake Day in Britain; think about special food days where you live

Text type: A recipe

Before you read

1. Look at the picture of the funny face sandwich. What do you think you need to make it?
2. Listen and read the recipe. CD1 46

Funny face sandwich

This sandwich is easy and fun to make. It's delicious, too!

To make this sandwich you need:

- one slice of bread
- three slices of cheese
- two slices of egg
- three olives
- one piece of carrot
- some salad

⚠ **Ask an adult to help you.**

Instructions:

First, put the slices of cheese on the slice of bread.

Then, add the eggs for eyes. Put an olive in the centre of each egg.

Now, add an olive for the nose and a piece of carrot for the mouth.

Finally, add the salad for the hair.

After you read

➔ Go to page 22 in your Activity Book.

Key learning outcomes: read and understand a recipe

1 Listen and number. Write and say. CD1 47

_____ _____ _____ _____ _____

_____ bread _____ _____ _____

2 Write the food in the correct column.

a	an	some
_____	egg	_____
_____	_____	_____

3 Cooperative learning Sing *Well done!* CD1 48

Key learning outcomes: review language in the unit
Language: food and *a* / *an* / *some*

1 Watch the video. Tick (✓) or cross (✗). Which toppings can you see?

2 Watch the video again. Read and circle.

1 First, you need flour and ***milk*** / ***water***.

2 Next, add the ***tomatoes*** / ***peppers***.

3 Now, add the ***cheese*** / ***onion***.

4 Cook the pizza for ***ten*** / ***twenty*** minutes.

3 Read, think and colour the stars.

Finding information online

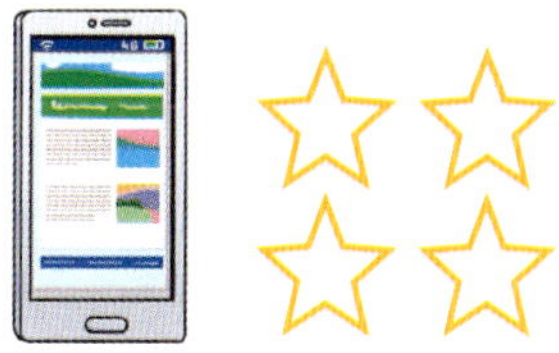

1 I look for information on my phone.

2 I look for information on my tablet.

3 I look for information on my computer.

4 I look for information in a book.

Key learning outcomes: watch and understand a video about recipes

21st **Digital skills:** finding recipes online

Unit 3 At the zoo

1 Listen and point. Sing *I'm a wild animal*.

CD1 50

I'm a wild animal. I'm dangerous!
I live in the jungle.
I've got four legs
And I'm orange and black.
Grrr! I'm a tiger!

I'm a wild animal. I'm dangerous!
I live in the grasslands.
I've got long hair
And I'm yellow and brown.
Grrr! I'm a lion!

I'm a wild animal. I'm dangerous!
I live in the water.
I've got a big mouth
And I'm long and green.
Snap! Snap! I'm a crocodile!

I'm a wild animal. I'm dangerous!
I live in the trees.
I've got long arms
And I climb and climb.
OO OO OO! I'm a monkey!

2 Read and stick the ten stickers. Listen and say the chant.

CD1 52

crocodile lion snake monkey penguin

Learning to learn **Spelling: go to page 35 in your Activity Book.**

Key learning outcomes: identify and say ten wild animals; sing a song about animals
Vocabulary: wild animals

1 Listen and repeat. Act out.

CD1 53

Grammar

Has it got big ears?

Yes, it has. No, it hasn't.

Have they got two legs?

Yes, they have. No, they haven't.

2 Listen and number.

CD1 54

1

elephant lizard giraffe hippo tiger

Key learning outcomes: use *Has it got …? / Have they got …?* and short answers

Grammar: *Has it got (big ears)? Yes, it has. Have they got (four legs)? No, they haven't.*

Before you read

1 Listen and read. Act out. CD1 55

The mysterious egg

Key learning outcomes: read, listen and understand a story about a mysterious egg

Language: *Has it got a long neck? No, it hasn't. This baby animal hasn't got big teeth. It's got feathers.*

Now watch the animated story!

After you read

2 **Values** **Read and write.**

Catch Help Bounce

______________ your friends and family.

1 Listen, point and say. CD2 1

body

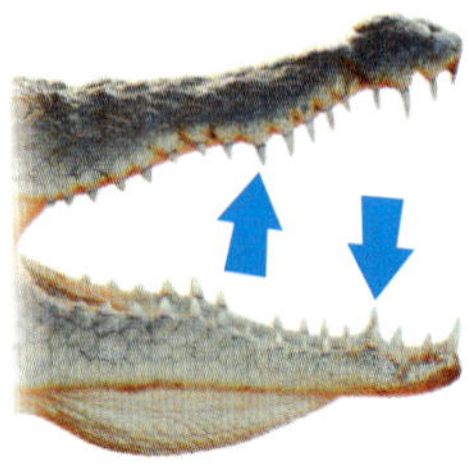
teeth

face

wings

tail

beak

2 Listen and point. Sing *The animal song*. CD2 2

Face, body, teeth and tail.
Beak and wings!

A tiger hasn't got a beak.
A tiger hasn't got wings.

Chorus

Monkeys haven't got a big face.
Monkeys haven't got a big body.

Chorus

A penguin hasn't got a long tail.
A penguin hasn't got teeth.

Chorus

3 Talk Partners Listen and repeat. Play a game. CD2 3

Key learning outcomes: describe and guess animals
Vocabulary: animal parts of the body **Grammar:** *It hasn't got (a beak). They haven't got (wings).*

1 Listen and say. CD2 5

2 Listen and number. CD2 6

3 Cooperative learning Sing *Let's take turns!* CD2 7

4 Talk Partners Make and play the game.

Teacher's Resource Bank: Unit 3

1 Listen and read. Answer.

CD2 8

1

Lots of different birds come into our garden. We put seeds and nuts on a table for the birds.

2

Hedgehogs come into the garden, too. We can see them at night.

3

Sometimes, a fox comes into the garden. It plays on the grass. We put water in a dish for it.

4

Squirrels climb the trees in our garden. They've got a long tail. They're naughty. They eat the bird food.

Think about your culture

Are there wild animals near your house?

Key learning outcomes: read about garden wildlife in Britain; think about wild animals where you live

Text type: **Fact files**

Before you read

1. What do you know about gorillas and polar bears? Think and say.

2. Listen and read the animal fact files. CD2 10

Animal Facts

Name: Gorilla

Habitat: Gorillas live in the rainforest.

Colour: Gorillas are black.

Size: Gorillas are big.

Characteristics: They've got black hair, small ears and very long arms. Gorillas haven't got a tail. They've got ten fingers and ten toes.

Food: They eat leaves and fruit. Some gorillas eat insects, too.

Animal Facts

Name: Polar bear

Habitat: Polar bears live on snow and ice.

Colour: Polar bears are white.

Size: Polar bears are big.

Characteristics: They've got white hair, a big body and four legs. Polar bears have got small ears and a small tail. They've got 42 teeth.

Food: They eat fish and meat.

After you read

Go to page **32** in your Activity Book.

Key learning outcomes: read and understand animal fact files

1 Listen and number. Write and say.

CD2 11

1 

crocodile

2 Read and write the animals.

1 They've got a long neck. They haven't got wings.

They're ______

2 They've got a beak and wings. They haven't got hair.

______

3 They've got a long body. They haven't got legs.

______

3 Cooperative learning Sing *Well done!*

CD2 12

Key learning outcomes: review language in the unit

Language: wild animals and *They've got …*

21 CHANNEL

Welcome back to Channel 21. Today's programme is about animals. What's your favourite animal?

1 Watch the video. Number the pictures.

1

2 Watch the video again. Read and tick (✓) or cross (✗).

1 Parrots have got small eyes. ✓

2 Parrots have got big, strong beaks. ☐

3 Parrots haven't got tails. ☐

4 Penguins haven't got beaks. ☐

3 Write the information in the correct place.

Sorting information

swim ~~fly~~ black and white eyes beak different colours

We can use a Venn Diagram to help us sort information.

1 parrots | 2 penguins

fly ______
______ ______ ______

PETS

Make a pets class book page

Learn

1 Listen, point and repeat. CD2 14

2 Ask your classmates. Tick (✓) or cross (✗).

Have you got any pets?

Yes, I have. I've got two dogs and a turtle.

Name										0

Plan your project

Plan your pets class book page. Go to page 36 in your Activity Book.

Key learning outcomes: identify and talk about pets
Language: *Have you got any pets? Yes, I have. I've got (two dogs and a turtle). No, I haven't.*

Create

Digital tip!
Take lots of photos of your pet and choose the best one.

1 Make your pets class book page.

1

Choose a photo of your pet. Add it to your document.

2

Type your text. Check your spelling.

Show and tell

2 **Cooperative learning** Sing *Listen to others.* CD2 15

3 Listen. Present your document to the class. CD2 16

It's lovely!

This is my dog. Its name is Bob.

Think about your project

Go to page 37 in your Activity Book.

Key learning outcomes: make and present your pets class book page
Language: *Its name is (Bob). Its favourite food is (meat).*

Unit 4 The nature trail

1 **Listen and point. Sing *I'm going on a nature trail*.** CD2 17

I'm going on a nature trail.
I'm having lots of fun!
I can run, run, run in the long, green grass.
I can jump, jump, jump in the leaves.

I'm going on a nature trail.
I'm having lots of fun!
I can walk, walk, walk in a big, dark forest.
I can climb, climb, climb a hill.

I'm going on a nature trail.
I'm having lots of fun!
I can swim, swim, swim in the deep, blue lake.
I can play, play, play in the sand.

2 **Read and stick the ten stickers. Listen and say the chant.** CD2 19

forest hill grass river leaves

Learning to learn → **Spelling: go to page 47 in your Activity Book.**

Key learning outcomes: identify and say ten features of a nature trail; sing a song about a nature trail
Vocabulary: features of a nature trail

1 Listen and repeat. Act out.

CD2 20

Grammar

What are you doing?

I'm climbing.

Are you running?

Yes, I am. No, I'm not.

2 Listen and tick (✓).

CD2 21

1

2

3

lake sand road path bridge

Before you read

1 **Listen and read. Act out.** CD2 22

What's Toby doing?

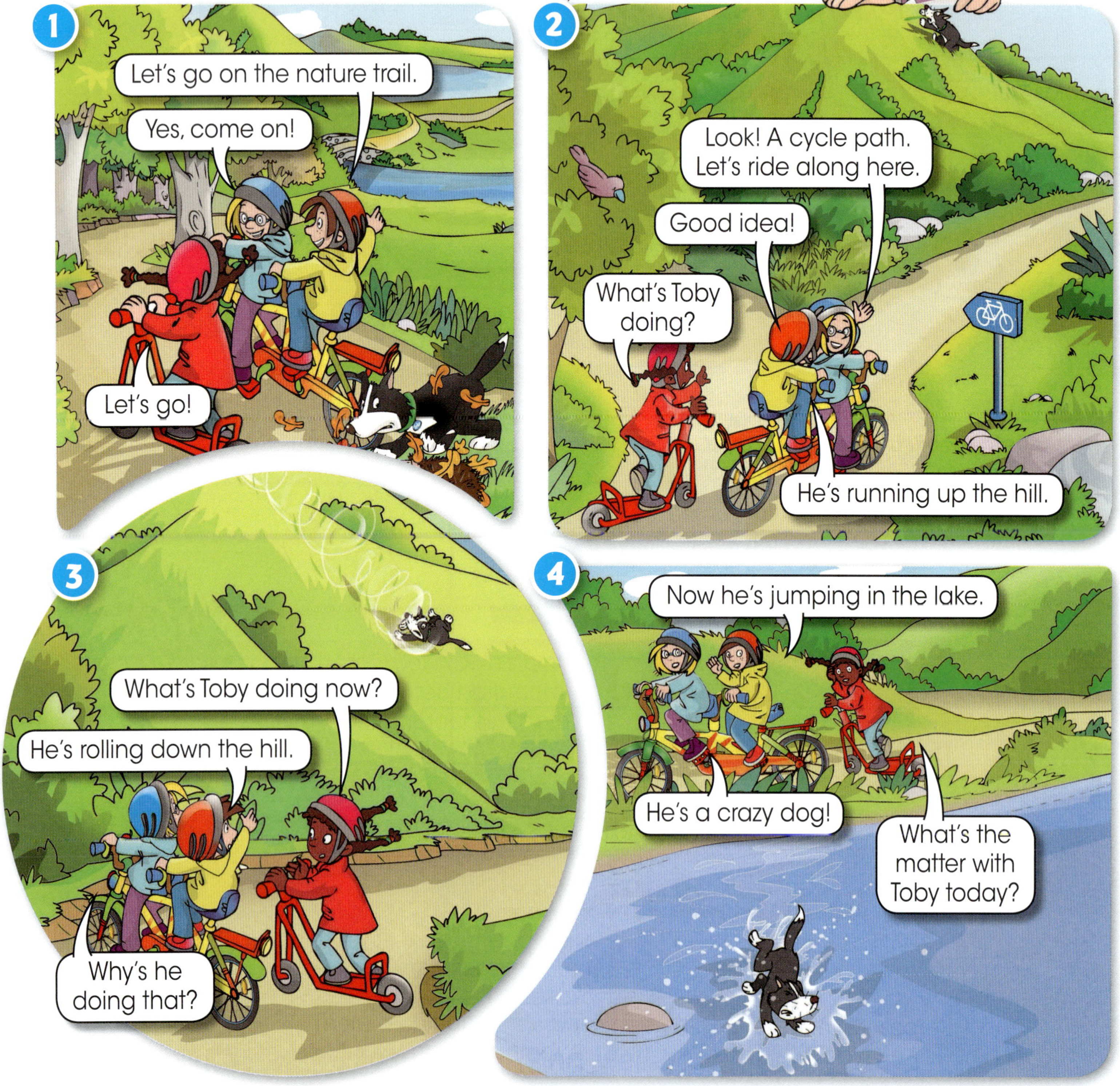

Key learning outcomes: read, listen and understand a story about Toby on a nature trail
Language: *What are you doing? What's Toby doing? He's running up the hill.*

Now watch the animated story!

After you read

2 **Values** **Read and write.**

see hear touch

Look at wild animals, but don't ________________.

 Vocabulary and Grammar

1 **Listen, point and say.** CD2 23

He's running **up** the hill.

He's running **down** the hill.

He's running **along** the path.

He's running **across** the bridge.

2 **Listen and point. Sing *What's he doing?*** CD2 24

What's he doing?
He's running up the hill.
Is he running down the hill?
No! He's running up the hill!

What's he doing?
He's sailing across the lake.
Is he sailing across the river?
No! He's sailing across the lake.

What's she doing?
She's walking along the path.
Is she walking along the road?
No! She's walking along the path!

What's she doing?
She's rolling down the hill!
CRASH!

3 **Talk Partners** **Listen and repeat. Play a game.** CD2 25

4 **Cooperative learning** **Sing *Calm down*.** CD2 26

Key learning outcomes: ask and answer questions to find out what people are doing
Vocabulary: prepositions of movement **Grammar:** *What's he / she doing? He's / She's (running ...).*

1 Listen and say. CD2 28

2 Listen and match. CD2 29

1 Sally
2 Ben
3 May

4 Sue
5 Bill
6 Nick

3 Talk Partners Make and play the game.

Teacher's Resource Bank: Unit 4

Key learning outcomes: play a communication game about a nature trail
Phonics: 'or' and 'al' spellings

Lesson 6 **British culture**

1 **Listen and read. Answer.** CD2 30

We sometimes go on school trips. Today, we're at a forest school. It's great fun!

1

We learn how to make a den from tree branches, twigs and leaves.

2

My favourite activity is exploring a tree. I can touch and smell the tree, but I can't see it.

3

We make mud pies and decorate them with flowers and leaves.

4

We go on a minibeast hunt. We count all the animals we see in the forest.

Think about your culture

What's your favourite outdoor activity?

Key learning outcomes: read about forest schools in Britain; think about your favourite outdoor activity

Text type: An adventure story

Before you read

1 What can you see in an adventure story? Circle and say.

a hero

a secret passage

Mum and Dad

an old bridge

a dark cave

a monkey

2 Listen and read the adventure story. CD2 32

After you read

Go to page 44 in your Activity Book.

Key learning outcomes: read and understand an adventure story

1 Listen and number. Write and say.

CD2 33

1

____ river ____ ____ ____

____ ____ ____ ____ ____

2 Talk Partners Listen. Act out. Ask and answer.

CD2 34

Are you climbing up a hill?

No, I'm not.

Are you swimming across a lake?

Yes, I am.

3 Cooperative learning Sing *Well done!*

CD2 35

Key learning outcomes: review language in the unit
Language: features of a nature trail and prepositions of movement

21 CHANNEL

Hello again. Today's programme is about nature. What's your favourite natural place?

1 **Watch the video. Tick (✓) or cross (✗). Are these places in the video?**

 ✓

2 **Watch the video again. Read and circle.**

1 They are walking along a ***road*** / ***path***.
2 The bridge goes ***over*** / ***along*** the river.
3 They are riding their ***horses*** / ***bikes***.
4 They're having a ***picnic*** / ***party***.

3 **Read and match.**

Looking after the environment

It's important to keep natural places clean and tidy.

1 Respect the signs.
2 Keep your dog on a lead.
3 Put your rubbish in the bin.
4 Don't pick wild flowers.
5 Don't feed wild animals.

Key learning outcomes: watch and understand a video about the environment
21st Living in the world: learning to look after the environment

Unit 5 The frozen lake

1 **Listen and point. Sing *We're going to the lake.*** CD2 37

We're going to the lake.
We're skating on the ice.
Wave and smile!
Are you ready?
Take a photo.
That's nice!

We're going to the lake.
We're making a snowman.
Wave and smile!
Are you ready?
Take a photo.
That's nice!

We're going to the lake.
We're drinking hot chocolate.
Wave and smile!
Are you ready?
Take a photo.
That's nice!

2 **Read and stick the ten stickers. Listen and say the chant.** CD2 39

drink skate wave smile dance

Learning to learn → **Spelling: go to page 57 in your Activity Book.**

Key learning outcomes: identify and say ten action verbs; sing a song about a frozen lake
Vocabulary: action verbs

1 Listen and repeat. Act out. CD2 40

Grammar

We're skating.

Are you dancing?

Yes, we are. No, we aren't.

2 Listen and number. CD2 41

make a snowman | eat | take a photo | play | listen to music

Before you read What are Jake and Molly making? Can you describe it?

1 Listen and read. Act out. CD2 42

The snowman

Key learning outcomes: read, listen and understand a story about a snowman
Language: *What are you doing? We're making a snowman. He's got a fat tummy.*

Now watch the animated story!

After you read

2 **Values** **Read and write.**

a scarf and a hat   a T-shirt and shorts   a swimsuit and goggles

Wear ______________________________

when you play out in the snow.

Values: wearing warm clothes when it's cold

1 Listen, point and say. CD2 43

a **fat** snowman

a **thin** snowman

a **short** snowman

a **tall** snowman

a **clean** snowman

a **dirty** snowman

2 Listen and point. Sing *What are they doing?* CD2 44

What are they doing?
They're playing in the snow.
Are they making a snowman?
I don't know.

He's got a dirty hat.
He's got a fat tummy.
His nose is a big, orange carrot.
He's got thin arms.
He's got a clean scarf.
His eyes are small, black stones.

What are they doing?
They're playing in the snow.
Are they making a snowman?
I think so!

3 Talk Partners Listen and repeat. Play a game. CD2 45

1

2

3

4

Key learning outcomes: describe and guess snowmen
Vocabulary: adjectives **Grammar:** *He's a (short) snowman. He's got a (dirty) hat.*

1 Listen and say. CD2 47

2 Listen and write *T* (true) or *F* (false). CD2 48

1

2

3

4

5

6

3 **Cooperative learning** Sing *Sharing is a good thing to do.* CD2 49

4 **Talk Partners** Make and play the game.

Teacher's Resource Bank: Unit 5

Key learning outcomes: play a communication game about what the snowmen are doing
Phonics: 'ow' and 'oa' spellings

1 Listen and read. Answer.

CD2 50

1

My brother and I go skating on the ice rink with our friends. Lots of people come here all year round.

2

There's a dry ski slope. We go skiing here.

3

We go tubing on the dry ski slope, too. It's great fun.

4

We can ride on a toboggan here, too. It's our favourite activity!

Think about your culture

What winter activities can you do where you live?

Key learning outcomes: read about winter activities in Britain; think about winter activities you can do where you live

Text type: **A fable**

Before you read

1 Look at the fable quickly. Find and circle the season words.

spring

summer

autumn

winter

2 Listen and read the fable. CD2 52

The ants and the grasshopper

It's summer. A grasshopper sees some ants. The grasshopper is singing and dancing. The ants are working.

"Hello, ants! What are you doing?" asks the grasshopper.

"We're working. We're collecting food for winter," answer the ants.

"You're silly!" says the grasshopper. "It's summer! Come and play."

"No," answer the ants. "Winter is coming."

In autumn, the grasshopper is still singing and dancing. The ants are still working.

"Hello, ants! What are you doing?" asks the grasshopper.

"We're working. We're collecting food for winter," answer the ants.

"You're so silly!" says the grasshopper.

In winter, the ants are happy. They're eating their food. The grasshopper is cold and hungry.

"I'm hungry!" says the grasshopper. "Can I have some food?"

"No," answer the ants. "Go and look for food in the snow!"

After you read

Go to page 54 in your Activity Book.

Key learning outcomes: read and understand a fable

1 Listen and number. Write and say. CD2 53

1

play

2 Talk Partners Listen. Act out. Ask and answer. CD2 54

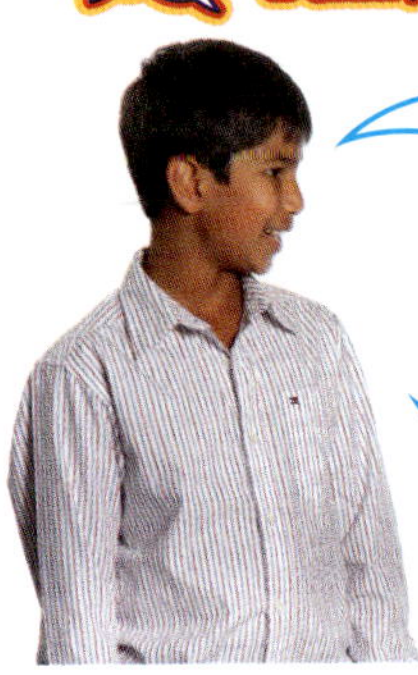

Are you skating on the ice?

No, we aren't.

Are you waving and smiling?

Yes, we are.

3 Cooperative learning Sing *Well done!* CD2 55

Key learning outcomes: review language in the unit
Language: action verbs and *Are you ...+ing?*

21 CHANNEL

Welcome back to Channel 21. Today's programme is making snowmen. Do you like playing in the snow?

1 **Watch the video. Number the pictures.**

1

2 **Watch the video again. Read and tick (✓) or cross (✗).**

1 The girl is making a snowman. ✓

2 All the snowmen have got hats.

3 The snowmen are the same.

4 All the snowmen are big.

3 **Read and think. Colour.**

very creative — not very creative

Being creative

Being creative can help you solve problems and have more fun. How creative are these snowmen? Order them.

1

2

3

4

Key learning outcomes: watch and understand a video about making snowmen

21st **Ways of thinking:** learning to be creative

Unit 6 All year round

1 Listen and point. Sing *What's your favourite season?*

CD3 1

What's your favourite season?
Is it spring?
Spring, when it's warm outside.
We smell flowers.
We plant seeds.
My favourite season is spring.

What's your favourite season?
Is it summer?
Summer, when it's hot outside.
We finish school.
We go to the beach.
My favourite season is summer.

What's your favourite season?
Is it autumn?
Autumn, when it's cool outside.
We eat chestnuts.
We celebrate Halloween.
My favourite season is autumn.

What's your favourite season?
Is it winter?
Winter, when it's cold outside.
We wear warm clothes.
We open presents.
My favourite season is winter.

spring

summer

autumn

winter

2 Read and stick the eight stickers. Listen and say the chant.

CD3 3

smell flowers

plant seeds

finish school

go to the beach

Learning to learn **Spelling: go to page 67 in your Activity Book.**

Key learning outcomes: identify and say eight seasonal activities; sing a song about seasons
Vocabulary: seasonal activities

1 Listen and repeat. Act out.

CD3 4

Grammar

What do you / they do in summer?
We / They go to the beach.

Do they celebrate Halloween?
Yes, they do. No, they don't.

2 Listen and tick (✓).

CD3 5

1

2

3

eat chestnuts | celebrate Halloween | wear warm clothes | open presents

Before you read

Which seasons can you see in the story?

1 Listen and read. Act out.

CD3 6

The four seasons

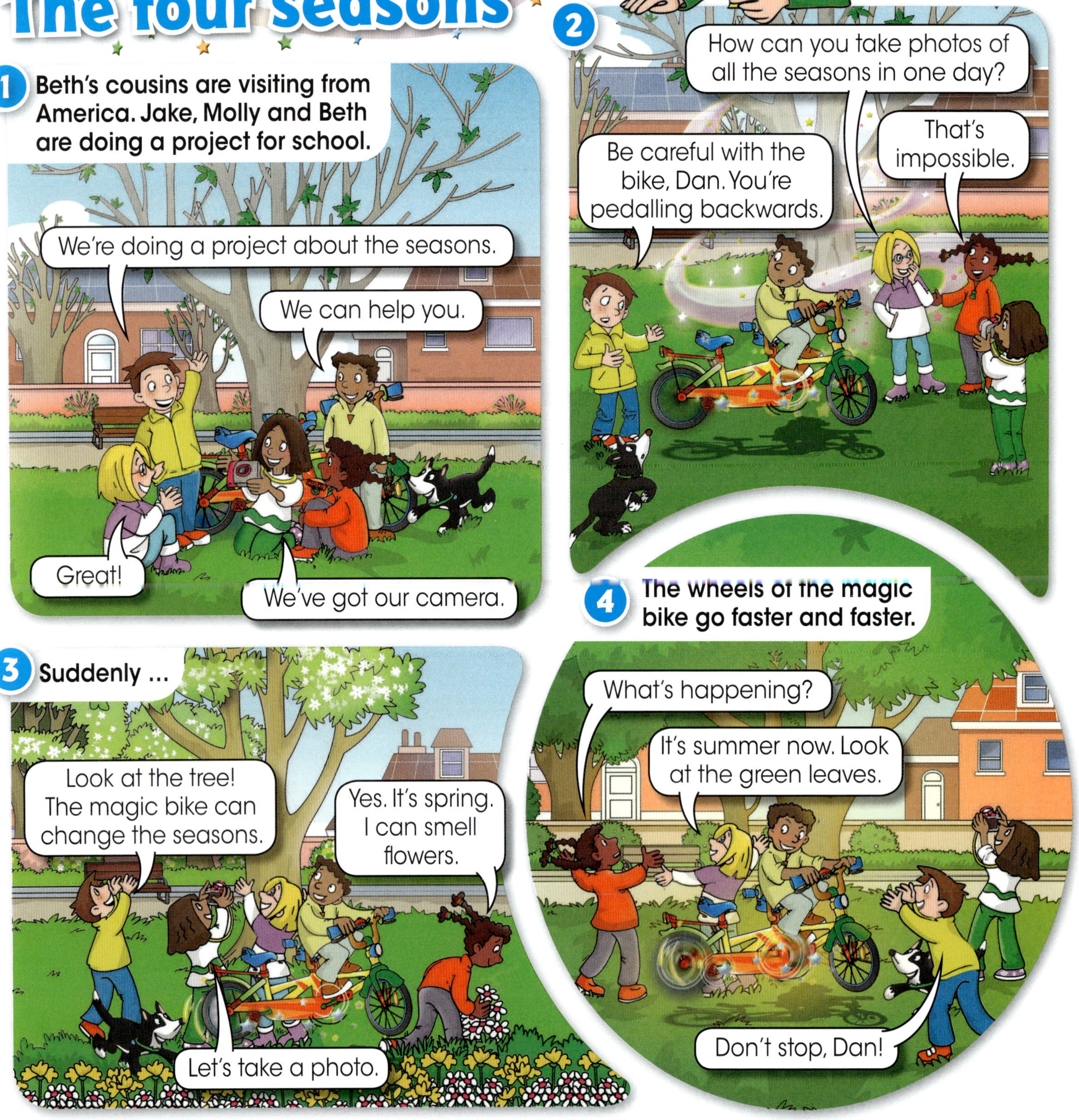

Key learning outcomes: read, listen and understand a story about the four seasons
Language: *Do you eat chestnuts in America, too? Yes, we do.*

5 

6 

7 

8 

After you read

Now watch the animated story!

2 **Values** **Read and write.**

stop help play

Working together, you can
_______________ your friends.

Values: working together

1 Listen, point and say. CD3 7

March

1st first	2nd second	3rd third	4th fourth	5th fifth	6th sixth	7th seventh
8th eighth	9th ninth	10th tenth	11th eleventh	12th twelfth	13th thirteenth	14th fourteenth
15th fifteenth	16th sixteenth	17th seventeenth	18th eighteenth	19th nineteenth	20th twentieth	21st twenty-first

2 Listen and point. Sing *When's your birthday?* CD3 8

My birthday is my favourite day.
Cake and presents. Hooray!

When's your birthday?
When's your birthday?
My birthday is on the ninth of May.
Do you want to come to my party?

When's your birthday?
When's your birthday?
My birthday is on the eighth of June.
Do you want to come to my party?

When's your birthday?
When's your birthday?
My birthday is on the twelfth of July.
Do you want to come to my party?

3 Talk Partners Listen and repeat. Ask and answer. CD3 9

Key learning outcomes: ask and answer about your birthday
Vocabulary: ordinal numbers **Grammar:** *When's your birthday? My birthday is on the (ninth) of (May).*

1 Listen and say. CD3 11

2 **Cooperative learning** Sing *We can do it!* CD3 12

3 Listen and write the names. CD3 13

January	February	March
________	________	________
April	**May**	**June**
________	Ann	________

4 **Talk Partners** Do a class survey.

Teacher's Resource Bank: Unit 6

When's your birthday?

My birthday is on the twenty-third of May. When's yours?

My birthday is on the thirtieth of November.

Which month has got the most birthdays?

Key learning outcomes: do a class survey about birthdays
Phonics: 'ur' and 'ir' spellings

1 Listen and read. Answer.

CD3 14

1 The first of April is April Fools' Day. We play jokes and we have a lot of fun!

2 Notting Hill Carnival is in August. There's a parade and people play the drums.

3 Remember, remember, the fifth of November! It's Bonfire Night. We make a 'guy' doll for a big bonfire.

4 On the twenty-fifth of December, it's Christmas. We eat turkey for Christmas lunch. We pull crackers and we wear paper hats, too.

Think about your culture

Do you have festivals in the four seasons? What festivals do you celebrate?

Key learning outcomes: read about seasonal festivals in Britain; think about seasonal festivals where you live

Text type: **A traditional rhyme**

Before you read

1 Look at the rhyme quickly. Find and circle the months.

February April June August October December
January March May July September November

2 Listen and read the rhyme. CD3 15

There are thirty days in September,
April, June and November.
All the rest have thirty-one,
Except for February alone.
And that has twenty-eight days clear,
And twenty-nine in each leap year!

After you read

Go to page 64 in your Activity Book.

Key learning outcomes: read and understand a traditional rhyme

1 Listen and number. Write and say. CD3 16

1 

open presents

2 Talk Partners Write. Ask and answer.

1 Do you eat chestnuts in spring? No, we don't.

2 Do you ________ in summer? ________

3 Do you ________ in autumn? ________

4 Do you ________ in winter? ________

3 Cooperative learning Sing *Well done!* CD3 17

Key learning outcomes: review language in the unit
Language: seasonal activities and *Do you …?*

21 CHANNEL

Hello again. Today's programme is about the seasons. What's your favourite season?

1 Watch the video. Tick (✓) or cross (✗). Are these activities in the video?

✓

2 Watch the video again. Read and circle.

1 They plant seeds in *summer* / *spring*.

2 They finish school in *summer* / *winter*.

3 They eat chestnuts in *spring* / *autumn*.

4 It's cold in *winter* / *summer*.

3 Do a survey. Ask your friends and write.

Doing a survey

You can do a survey. Ask your friends, 'What's your favourite season?'

	Spring	Summer	Autumn	Winter
Friend 1 ________				
Friend 2 ________				
Friend 3 ________				

Key learning outcomes: watch and understand a video about seasons

21st **Ways of working:** learning to do a survey

JOBS

Make a jobs poster

Learn

1 Listen, point and repeat. CD3 20

1

2

3

4

5

6

7

8

9

10

2 Listen and number. Listen and repeat. CD3 21

A teacher teaches children.

A doctor helps people.

A vet helps animals.

1

A police officer wears a uniform.

Plan your project

Plan your jobs poster.
Go to page 68 in your Activity Book.

A firefighter puts out fires.

A pilot flies a plane.

Key learning outcomes: identify and talk about jobs
Language: *A doctor helps people. A pilot flies a plane.*

Create

1 Read. Make your jobs poster.

1

Draw, colour and write about the job.

2

Make and decorate the poster.

Digital tip!

Use the Internet to look for more information about the job.

Show and tell

2 Cooperative learning Sing *It's fun to work together!* CD3 22

3 Listen. Present your jobs poster to the class.
Make a class jobs wall display with all the posters. CD3 23

She's a vet.

She wears a white coat.

She helps animals.

Think about your project

Go to page 69 in your Activity Book.

Key learning outcomes: make a jobs poster; present a class jobs wall display
Language: *She's a (vet). She (wears a white coat). She (helps animals).*

Unit 7 My house

1 Listen and point. Sing *There's a mouse in my house!*

CD3 24

There's a mouse in my house!
Where can it be?
Is it in the living room, watching TV?
Is it in the bathroom, having a shower?
Is it in the garden, watering the flowers?

There's a mouse in my house!
Where can it be?
Is it in the kitchen, eating all the food?
Is it in the hall, playing in my shoes?

There's a mouse in my house!
Where can it be?
Is it in the dining room, eating all the bread?
Is it in the bedroom, under the bed?

There's a mouse in my house!
Where can it be?
Is it in the garage, running on the floor?
Run outside little mouse!
Quick, shut the door!

2 Read and stick the ten stickers. Listen and say the chant.

CD3 26

flat

house

living room

kitchen

bathroom

Learning to learn → **Spelling: go to page 79 in your Activity Book.**

Key learning outcomes: identify and say ten rooms in the house; sing a song about a mouse
Vocabulary: rooms in the house

1 Listen and repeat. Act out. CD3 27

Grammar

There's a kitchen.

There are three bedrooms.

There isn't a garden.

There aren't any plants.

2 Listen and write *a, b, c* or *d*. CD3 28

1

2

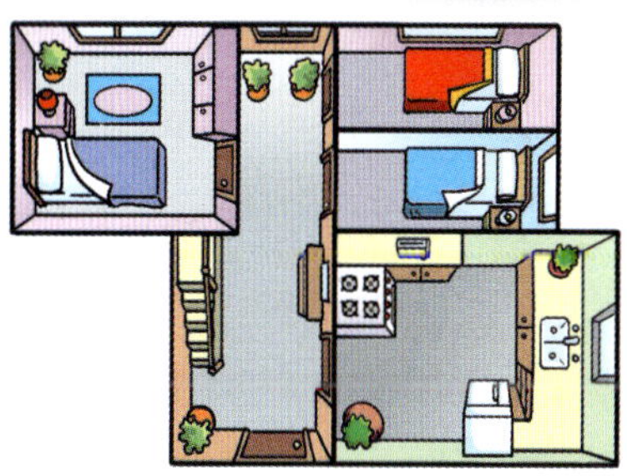

a

3

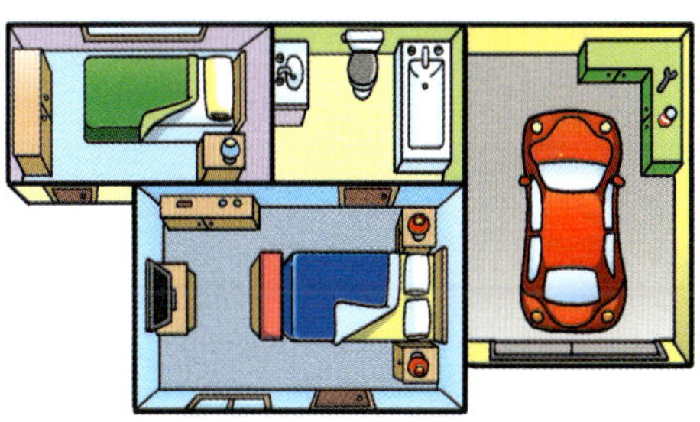

4

bedroom dining room hall garden garage

Key learning outcomes: use *There's a / There are / There isn't a / There aren't any*

Grammar: *There's a / There isn't a (hall). There are / There aren't any (plants).*

Before you read Which rooms can you see in the story?

1 Listen and read. Act out. CD3 29

The haunted house

Key learning outcomes: read, listen and understand a story about a haunted house
Language: *There's a haunted bedroom. There aren't any skeletons.*

Now watch the animated story!

After you read

2 **Values** **Read and write.**

kind   happy   tired

Be ______________ to your friends when they are scared.

7 Lesson 4 **Vocabulary and Grammar**

1 **Listen, point and say.** CD3 30

camera

clock

radio

box

phone

watch

2 **Listen and point. Sing *What a mess!*** CD3 31

3 **Talk Partners** **Listen and repeat. Ask and answer.** CD3 32

Key learning outcomes: ask and answer about who objects belong to
Vocabulary: objects **Grammar:** *Whose is this (watch)? It's mine / yours / his / hers.*

1 Listen and say. CD3 34

ow – ou – ow – ou. A brown cow and a loud mouse run around the house.

2 Listen and match. CD3 35

3 Talk Partners Make and play the game.

Teacher's Resource Bank: Unit 7

Key learning outcomes: play a communication game about where objects are
Phonics: 'ow' and 'ou' spellings

1 Listen and read. Answer.

CD3 36

My brother and I have got our own bedrooms. His is big. Mine is small, but I like it. Come and see.

1

We live in a house with a big garden. Our bedrooms are upstairs.

2

I've got a lot of books, so there's a bookcase in my bedroom. I love music. I've got a guitar and drums.

3

I've got a sticker collection in my bedroom. Today, I'm making a book of animal stickers with Alice.

4

Sometimes, we have a pyjama party with our friends. We play board games and we listen to pop music.

Think about your culture

What have you got in your bedroom?

Key learning outcomes: read about bedrooms in Britain; think about what you've got in your bedroom

Text type: **A play script**

Before you read

1 **What's in the play? Look and circle.**

a pumpkin

a shoe

a clock

a dragon

some mice

a fairy godmother

2 **Listen and read the play script.** CD3 38

Cinderella

Scene 1

Cinderella lives in a big house with her two wicked sisters. There are twenty bedrooms, seventeen bathrooms and two kitchens.

Sister 1: Tidy up, Cinderella!
Cinderella: Yes, of course. Whose is this phone?
Sister 2: It's mine.

Scene 2

Poor Cinderella. She's cleaning the house. There's a party tonight, but she can't go.

Cinderella: I'm sad. My dress is old.
Fairy Godmother: Here's a new dress. These mice can be horses. This pumpkin can be a car. These shoes are made of glass. You can go to the party now!

Scene 3

Prince: Do you want to dance?
Cinderella: Yes, please.
Cinderella: Oh no! It's midnight.
Prince: Come back!

Cinderella runs away. Her shoe falls off. The horses are mice again. The car is a pumpkin again. Her dress is old again.

Scene 4

The next day, Cinderella is cleaning the house. The prince visits.

Prince: Whose is this shoe?
Sisters 1 and 2: It's mine!
Prince: Cinderella. Is it yours?
Cinderella: Yes, it's mine. Thank you.

The Prince and Cinderella get married and live happily ever after.

After you read

Go to page 76 in your Activity Book.

1 Listen and number. Write and say.

CD3 39

1

house

2 Look at Activity 1. Write true sentences.

1 There aren't ______ six chairs in the dining room.

2 ______ a piano in the living room.

3 ______ a clock in the hall.

4 ______ any animals in the garden.

5 ______.

6 ______.

3 Cooperative learning Sing *Well done!*

CD3 40

Key learning outcomes: review language in the unit
Language: rooms and *There's / There are / There isn't / There aren't*

Welcome back to Channel 21. Today's programme is about unusual houses. What's your house like?

1 Watch the video. Number the pictures.

2 Watch the video again. Read and tick (✓) or cross (✗).

1 There's a boat with a garden. ✓
2 There's a small castle.
3 There aren't any red flats.
4 There are lots of toys in the bedroom.

3 Read and circle.

Helping at home

It's important to tidy up.

1 Put the books on the ***floor*** / ***shelf***.
2 Put the toys in the ***pencil case*** / ***box***.
3 Put the clock on the ***table*** / ***bed***.
4 Put the shoes in the ***box*** / ***cupboard***.

Unit 8 All around the town

1 **Listen and point. Sing** *All around the town*. CD3 42

All around the town.
All around the town.
Let's go exploring,
All around the town.

Is there a baker's?
Is there a bank?
Is there a police station?

Chorus

Is there a post office?
Is there a chemist's?
Is there a fire station?

Chorus

Is there a bus station?
Is there a museum?
Is there a train station?

Chorus

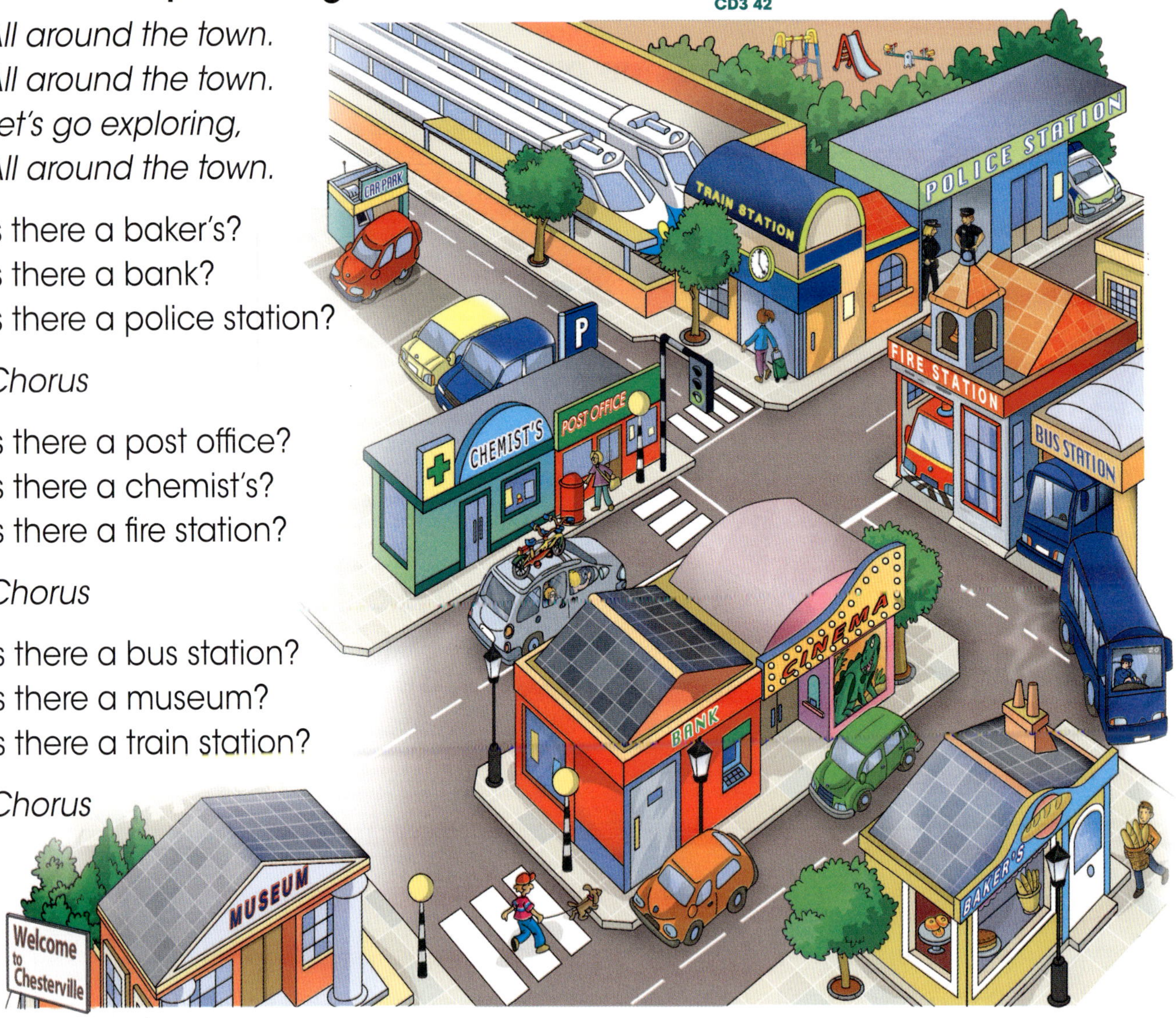

2 **Read and stick the ten stickers. Listen and say the chant.** CD3 44

baker's | fire station | police station | car park | bank

Learning to learn → **Spelling: go to page 89 in your Activity Book.**

Key learning outcomes: identify and say ten places in a town; sing a song about a town
Vocabulary: places in a town

1 Listen and repeat. Act out.

CD3 45

Grammar

Is there a cinema?

Yes, there is. No, there isn't.

Are there any museums?

Yes, there are. No, there aren't.

2 Listen and number.

CD3 46

a

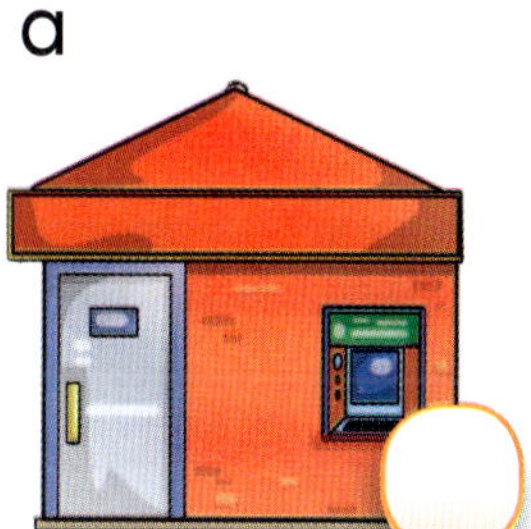

b

c

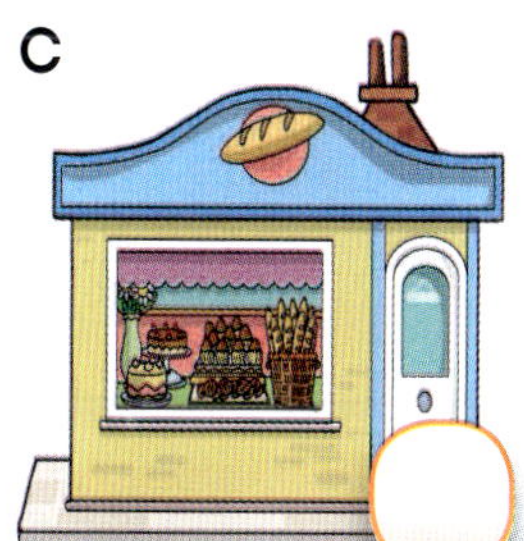

d

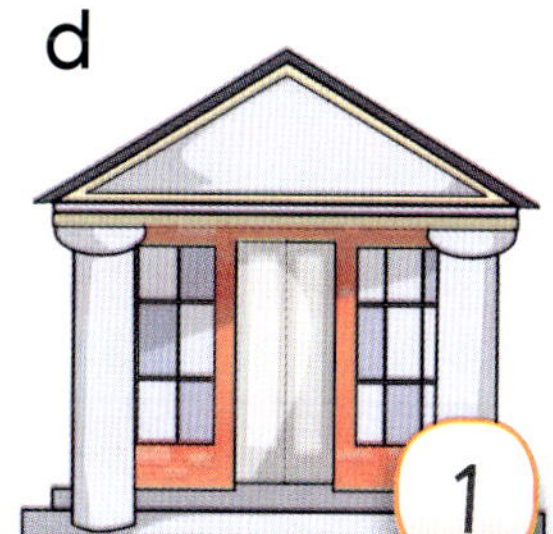

e

post office | chemist's | bus station | train station | museum

Key learning outcomes: use *Is there a …? / Are there any …?* and short answers
Grammar: *Is there a (cinema)? Yes, there is. Are there any (museums)? No, there aren't.*

Before you read

1 Listen and read. Act out. CD3 47

The dark night

Key learning outcomes: read, listen and understand a story about a dark night
Language: *Is there a baker's? Are there any banks near here? Turn right here.*

After you read

Now watch the animated story!

2 **Values** **Read and write.**

remember forget stop

Try to ______________ where you put your things.

Values: remembering where you put your things

1 Listen, point and say. CD3 48

go straight on

turn left

turn right

from … to …

2 Listen and point. Sing *Which way do I go?* CD3 49

How do I get to the post office?
Which way do I go?
How do I get from here to there?
Go straight on.
There's the post office.

How do I get to the fire station?
Which way do I go?
How do I get from here to there?
Turn left.
There's the fire station.

How do I get to the train station?
Which way do I go?
How do I get from here to there?
Turn right.
There's the train station.

3 Talk Partners Listen and repeat. Act out. CD3 50

Key learning outcomes: ask for and give directions
Vocabulary: directions **Grammar:** *How do I get to the (post office)? Turn (left). Go straight on.*

1 Listen and say. CD4 1

2 Listen and draw lines. Use different colours. CD4 2

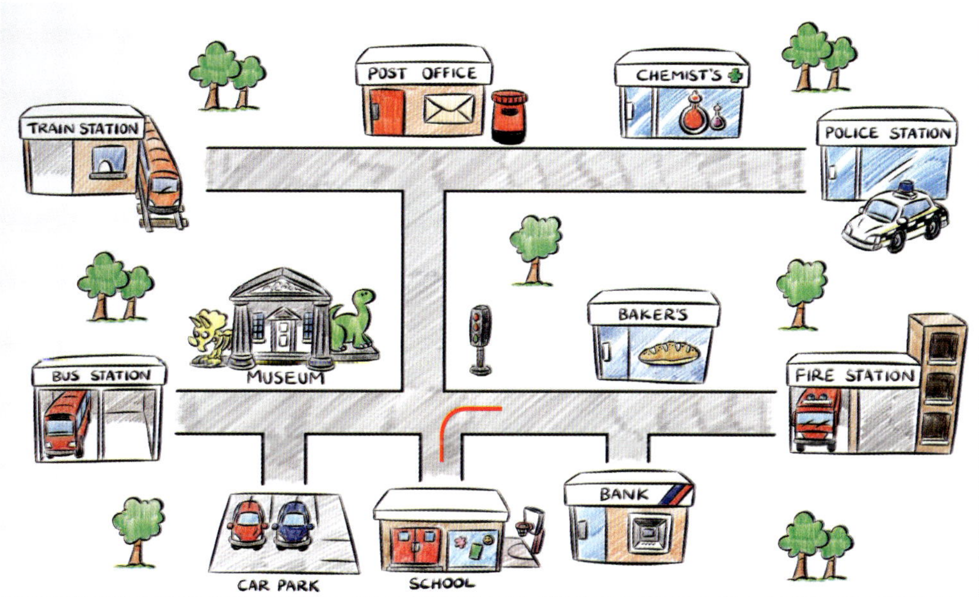

3 Talk Partners Make and play the game.

Teacher's Resource Bank: Unit 8

1 Listen and read. Answer.

CD4 3

Our mum and dad help people. Our mum is a police officer and our dad is a firefighter.

1

Our dad drives a big, red fire engine. It's got big wheels and a loud siren.

2

He wears a yellow helmet and a safety uniform.

3

Our mum is a police officer. She sometimes rides a bike around the town. She helps people.

4

The emergency telephone number in Britain is 999. Call this number if you need a doctor, a firefighter or a police officer.

Think about your culture

Do you know the emergency telephone number in your country?

Key learning outcomes: read about the emergency services in Britain; think about the emergency telephone number where you live

Text type: An invitation

Before you read

1 What can you see on the invitation? Tick (✓).

a name ✓ | a day | a photo | a date | a map

a phone number | directions | a season

2 Listen and read the invitation. CD4 5

After you read

Go to page 86 in your Activity Book.

1 Listen and number. Write and say. CD4 6

___ ___ ___

___ ___ ___ ___

1

___ ___ post office

2 Talk Partners Listen. Look at Activity 1. Ask and answer. CD4 7

Are there any museums in your town?

Yes, there are.

Is there a train station?

No, there isn't.

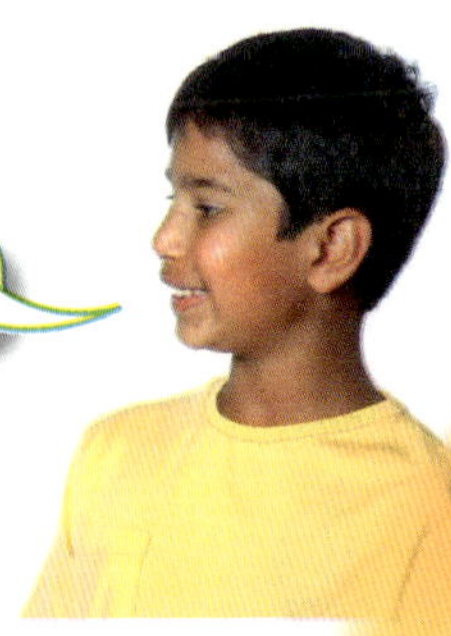

3 Cooperative learning Sing *Well done!* CD4 08

Key learning outcomes: review language in the unit
Language: places in a town and *Is there a …?*

21 CHANNEL

Hello again. Today's programme is about important places in town. What important places are there in your town?

1 Watch the video. Tick (✓) or cross (✗). Which places are in the video?

☐ ☐ ☐ ✓

2 Watch the video again. Read and answer.

1 What's the police officer doing?

2 Where can you buy stamps?

3 Where's the train station?

4 Where can you cross the road?

3 Read and think. Tick (✓) or cross (✗).

Crossing the road safely

It's important to stop, look, listen and think before you cross the road.

1 Run across the road. ☐

2 Wait for the red man. ☐

3 Look and listen when you cross the road. ☐

4 Look for a zebra crossing. ☐

Key learning outcomes: watch and understand a video about road safety

21st Living in the world: learn to cross the road safely

Unit 9

Holiday fun

1 **Listen and point. Sing *We're on holiday*.** CD4 10

We're on holiday.
We're having a great time.
There are lots of things to do.

We're on holiday.
We're having a great time.
Let's go to the circus.
Let's go to the science museum
And see animals
In the safari park.

Chorus

We're on holiday.
We're having a great time.
Let's go to the theatre.
Let's go to the chocolate factory
And see dolphins
In the aquarium.

Chorus

2 **Read and stick the ten stickers. Listen and say the chant.** CD4 12

castle | circus | science museum | water park | funfair

Learning to learn → **Spelling: go to page 99 in your Activity Book.**

Key learning outcomes: identify and say ten holiday places; sing a song about a holiday
Vocabulary: holiday places

1 Listen and repeat. Act out.

CD4 13

Grammar

Where were you yesterday?

I was at the circus.

2 Listen and match.

CD4 14

1

2

3

a

b

c

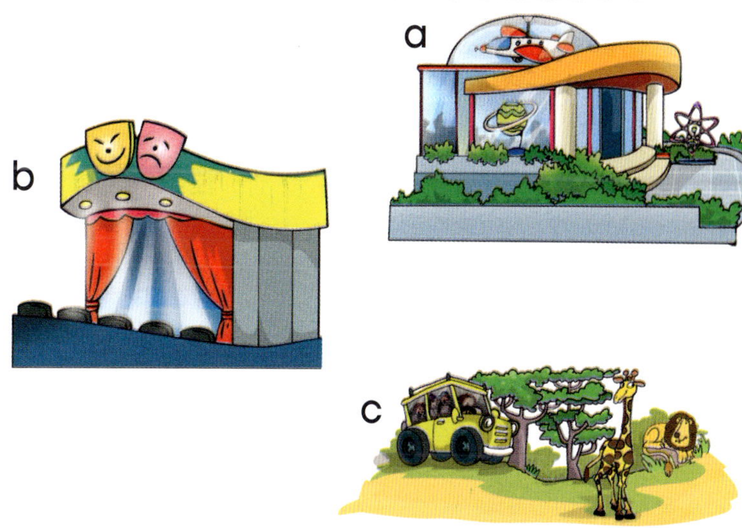

chocolate factory | aquarium | sports centre | safari park | theatre

Before you read

Where do we go on a day trip?

1 **Listen and read. Act out.** CD4 15

The magic trip

Key learning outcomes: read, listen and understand a story about a magic trip

Language: *Where were you? We were at (a chocolate factory).*

After you read

Now watch the animated story!

2 **Values** Read and write.

play   watch TV   go skiing

In summer, ________________ outside with your friends.

Values: playing outside with your friends

1 Listen, point and say. CD4 16

man

men

woman

women

child

children

2 Listen and point. Sing *Who's that?* CD4 17

Who's that woman in your photo?
She's got blue eyes
And long blonde hair.
She's my aunt. Here she is
On holiday with me.

Who are those children in your photo?
They've got green eyes
And short black hair.
They're my cousins. Here they are
On holiday with me.

Who's that man in your photo?
He's got brown eyes
And short brown hair.
He's my uncle. Here he is
On holiday with me.

3 Talk Partners Listen and repeat. Ask and answer. CD4 18

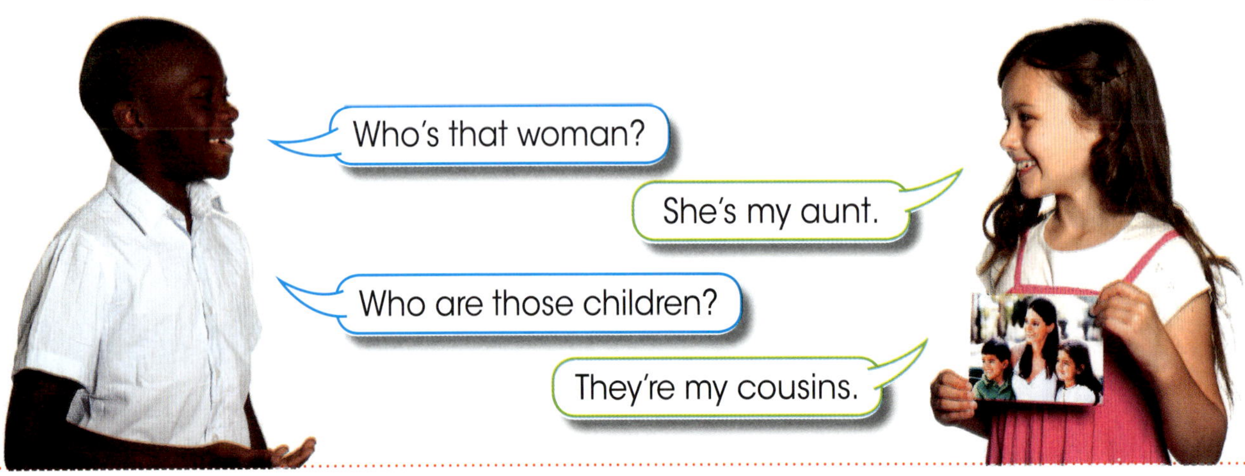

Key learning outcomes: ask and answer about people **Vocabulary:** irregular plural nouns **Grammar:** *Who's that … ? He's / She's … Who are those … ? They're …*

1 Listen and say. CD4 20

2 Listen and match. CD4 21

1 father

2 brother

3 grandmother

4 cousin

5 aunt

6 grandfather

3 Talk Partners Make and play the game.

Teacher's Resource Bank: Unit 9

Key learning outcomes: play a communication game about where you were
Phonics: 'ear' and 'air' spellings

1 Listen and read. Answer.

CD4 22

It's the summer holidays. Yesterday, we were at Blenheim Palace. There are lots of fun things to do in the gardens.

1

We love the maze. It's very big. We can play hide and seek here. Where are Dad and Anna?

2

There are some giant games! In this photo, we're playing giant chess. Mum and Tom are winning.

3

Our favourite place is the arts and crafts studio. In this photo, we're painting a plate and a cup for Dad. It's his birthday on the fourteenth of August.

4

There's a butterfly house here, too. We can see butterflies from all around the world. They're beautiful.

Think about your culture

What do you do in the summer holidays?

Key learning outcomes: read about summer holidays in Britain; think about what you do in your summer holidays

Text type: A diary

Before you read

1 Look at the diary quickly. Find and circle the days.

Monday Saturday Tuesday Thursday Wednesday Friday Sunday

2 Listen and read the diary. CD4 24

My diary

Yesterday was Saturday. It was sunny and hot. I was at the circus all day with my mum and dad and my sisters. It was great!

Here's my ticket.

Here's a photo of my big sister with a clown.

Here's my little sister with a man on stilts. He's very tall.

Yesterday was Sunday. It was cold and cloudy. I was at the funfair with my cousins. It was fantastic! It was my cousin's birthday.

Here he is with his badge.

My favourite ride was the roller coaster. It was very fast!

Here's my ticket.

And here's a photo of me and my aunt.

After you read

Go to page 96 in your Activity Book.

Key learning outcomes: read and understand a diary

1 Listen and number. Write and say.

CD4 25

1

science museum

2 Talk Partners Listen. Make a fun holiday diary. Ask and answer.

CD4 26

Where were you on Monday?

I was at the castle.

Where were you on Tuesday?

I was at the safari park.

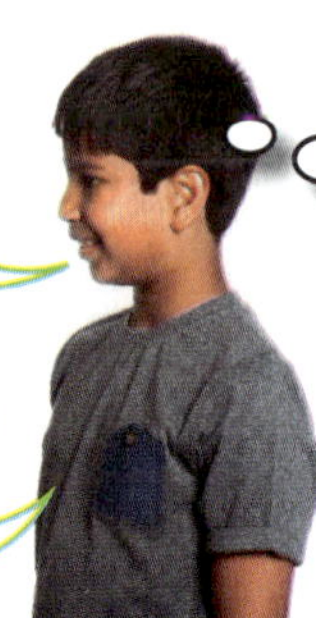

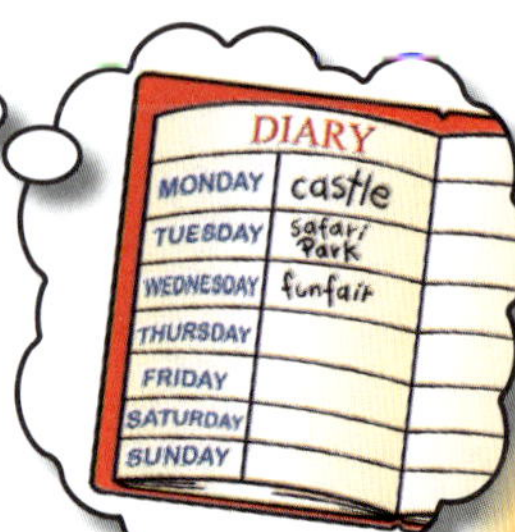

3 Cooperative learning Sing *Well done!*

CD4 27

Key learning outcomes: review language in the unit

Language: holiday places and *I was* …

21 CHANNEL

Welcome back to Channel 21. Today's programme is about having fun at the weekend. What do you do at the weekend?

1 Watch the video. Number the pictures.

2 Watch the video again. Read and tick (✓) or cross (✗).

1 Tom was at the funfair. ✓
2 Dan was at the circus.
3 Ben was at the forest.
4 Sue was at the safari park.

3 Read and circle.

Using a digital camera

Taking photos helps you to remember fun days out!

1 This is my aunt. She was at the ***water park*** / ***aquarium***.

2 These are my cousins. They were at the ***castle*** / ***circus***.

3 This is my uncle. He was at the ***theatre*** / ***safari park***.

4 These are my sisters. They were at the ***chocolate factory*** / ***sports centre***.

Key learning outcomes: watch and understand a video about weekend activities
21st **Digital skills:** learn to use a digital camera

TIME

Make a clock and talk about your daily routine

Learn

1 Listen, point and repeat. CD4 29

1 

2 

3 

4 

2 Listen. Play *Find the clock*. CD4 30

It's a quarter to nine.

It's number four. It's my turn.

3 Listen, point and repeat. CD4 31

1 

I get up at half past seven.

2 

I get dressed at a quarter to eight.

3 

I have breakfast at a quarter past eight.

4 

I go to school at nine o'clock.

5 

I play at half past six.

6 

I go to bed at half past nine.

Plan your project

Practise the time. Go to page 100 in your Activity Book.

Key learning outcomes: identify and talk about times

Language: *It's (eight o'clock). I (get up) at (half past seven).*

Create

1 Read. Make your clock.

1

Decorate the clock. Cut out the clock and the two hands.

2

Attach the two hands with a butterfly clip.

Show and tell

2 Cooperative learning Sing *Listen to others.* CD4 32

3 Listen. Tell the class about your day. CD4 33

Digital tip!

Record your presentation on video.

Think about your project

Go to page 101 in your Activity Book.

Key learning outcomes: make a clock; tell the class about your daily routine
Language: *I (have breakfast) at (half past eight).*

Harvest Festival

We celebrate Harvest Festival in autumn.

1 Listen and read. CD4 34

1 British children celebrate Harvest Festival in autumn.

2 We say thank you for all the food that grows in summer.

3 We make big baskets of fruit and vegetables.

2 Listen and read. Match. Say the harvest poem. CD4 35

Summer is over.
Autumn is here.

It's Harvest Festival.
Give a cheer!

The harvest moon
is big and round.

We say 'Thank you' for the food
that grows in the ground.

Think about your culture

Do you celebrate Harvest Festival?

Teacher's Resource Bank: Festivals

Key learning outcomes: say a harvest poem

Language: *We celebrate (Harvest Festival). We make (big baskets).*

Carnival

1 Listen and read. Say the carnival rhyme. CD4 36

Put on your **costume**.

Paint your face.

Wear a **wig** or a hat,

A **mask** or a **cape**.

Join the **parade**.

Dance and have fun.

It's time for the competition.

Hooray! I won!

2 Read the rhyme again. Find the names of these things in the rhyme.

1 

2 

3 

4 

5 

3 Listen and number. CD4 37

Think about your culture

What do you do for carnival?

Teacher's Resource Bank: Festivals

Key learning outcomes: say a carnival rhyme

Language: *Put on (your costume). Paint (your face). Wear (a wig).*

Listening

1 **Listen and tick (✓). There is one example.** CD4 38

1 What is Anna's hobby?

A 

B 

C 

2 What is Pat's favourite sport?

A 

B 

C 

3 Which is Bill?

A 

B 

C 

Speaking

2 **Listen and repeat. Ask and answer.** CD4 39

Do you like hockey?

Yes, I do.

Do you go skateboarding?

Yes, I do. I go skateboarding on Saturday.

What's your favourite sport?

My favourite sport is football.

Watch the external exams video

Key learning outcomes: practise for the Starters Listening Part 3 and Speaking Part 4

Listening

1 Read the questions. Listen and write a name or a number. There is one example. CD4 40

1 What is the boy's name? Alex

2 What is the girl's name? __________

3 How old is the boy? __________

4 How old is the girl? __________

5 How many apples are there? __________

6 What is the dog's name? __________

Speaking

2 Listen and point. Ask and answer. CD4 41

What are these?

They're potatoes.

Do you have potatoes for lunch?

Yes, I do.

Watch the external exams video

Key learning outcomes: practise for the Starters Listening Part 2 and Speaking Part 3

Listening

1 Listen and draw lines. There is one example. CD4 42

Mark Alice May

Lucy Tom Alex Hugo

Speaking

2 Listen and point. Ask and answer. CD4 43

What are these?

They're elephants.

What colour are they?

They're grey.

Watch the external exams video

Key learning outcomes: practise for the Starters Listening Part 1 and Speaking Part 3

Listening

1 **Read the questions. Listen and write a name or a number. There is one example.** CD4 44

1 What is the boy's name? Bill
2 What is the girl's name? ______
3 How many dogs has the boy got? ______
4 How many cats has the girl got? ______
5 What is the name of the boy's favourite animal? ______

Speaking

2 **Listen. Ask and answer.** CD4 45

Watch the external exams video

Listening

1 Listen and tick (✓). There is one example.

CD4 46

1 What is Dad doing?

A 
B 
C 

2 Which is Lucy?

A 
B 
C 

3 What are Ann and Tom doing?

A 
B 
C 

Speaking

2 Listen and point. Ask and answer.

CD4 47

Watch the external exams video

Key learning outcomes: practise for the Starters Listening Part 3 and Speaking Part 3

Listening

1 Listen and tick (✓). There is one example.

CD4 48

1 Where are Hugo and Jill?

A

B

✓
C

2 Which is Eva?

A

B

C

3 What are Tony and Sue doing?

A

B

C

Speaking

2 Listen and repeat. Ask and answer.

CD4 49

How old are you?

I'm seven.

When's your birthday?

My birthday is on the second of August.

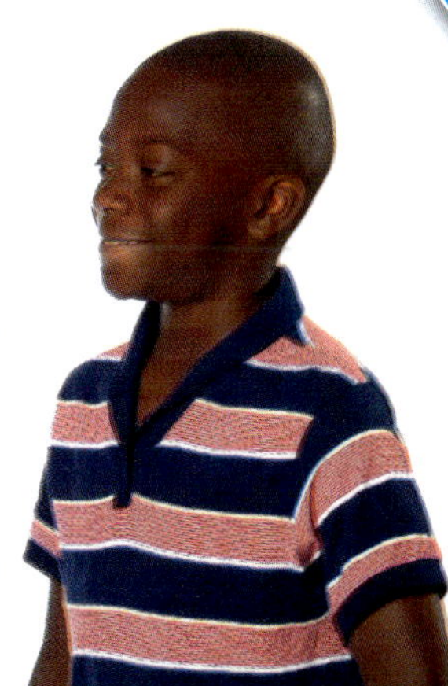

Watch the external exams video

Key learning outcomes: practise for the Starters Listening Part 3 and Speaking Part 4

Listening

1 Listen and colour. There is one example.

CD4 50

Speaking

2 Listen and repeat. Ask and answer.

CD4 51

Do you live in a house or a flat?

I live in a flat.

What's your favourite room?

My favourite room is my bedroom.

What's in your bedroom?

There's a bed and there are lots of posters.

Watch the external exams video

posters computer table chair lamp clock bookcase

Key learning outcomes: practise for the Starters Listening Part 4 and Speaking Part 4

Listening

1 Listen and colour. There is one example. CD4 52

Speaking

2 Listen and point. Ask and answer. CD4 53

Watch the external exams video

Key learning outcomes: practise for the Starters Listening Part 4 and Speaking Part 3

Listening

1 Listen and draw lines. There is one example. CD4 54

Sue Hugo Anna Tom

Eva Tony Bill

Speaking

2 Listen and repeat. Ask and answer. CD4 55

Have you got any brothers or sisters?

Yes. I've got one brother and one sister.

What's your sister's name?

Her name's Anna.

Watch the external exams video

Key learning outcomes: practise for the Starters Listening Part 1 and Speaking Part 4

Speaking

Speaking

cut

External Exams Syllabus

Unit	Cambridge Exam Practice (Pupil's Book)	Cambridge Exam Practice (Activity Book)	Trinity Exam practice (Teacher's Resource Bank)
Unit 1	**Pre A1 Starters Listening Part 3** Task: Multiple choice picture cloze **Pre A1 Starters Speaking Part 4** Task: Answering questions to give personal information	**Pre A1 Starters Reading and Writing Part 4** Task: Text cloze **Pre A1 Starters Reading and Writing Part 2** Task: Writing yes / no answers	**Grades 2 and 3** Asking simple questions and giving personal information
Unit 2	**Pre A1 Starters Listening Part 2** Task: Writing names and numbers **Pre A1 Starters Speaking Part 3** Task: Answering questions about small pictures	**Pre A1 Starters Reading and Writing Part 3** Task: Spelling words **Pre A1 Starters Reading and Writing Part 1** Task: Putting tick / cross answers	**Grades 2 and 3** Identifying and naming numbers and understanding simple instructions
Unit 3	**Pre A1 Starters Listening Part 1** Task: Matching names and children **Pre A1 Starters Speaking Part 3** Task: Answering questions about small pictures	**Pre A1 Starters Reading and Writing Part 4** Task: Text cloze **Pre A1 Starters Reading and Writing Part 3** Task: Spelling words	**Grades 2 and 3** Stating simple facts and answering simple questions
Unit 4	**Pre A1 Starters Listening Part 2** Task: Writing names and numbers **Pre A1 Starters Speaking Part 2** Task: Answering questions and talking about a big picture	**Pre A1 Starters Reading and Writing Part 2** Task: Writing yes / no answers **Pre A1 Starters Reading and Writing Part 5** Task: Writing one word answers	**Grades 2 and 3** Asking and answering simple questions and indicating the position of objects
Unit 5	**Pre A1 Starters Listening Part 3** Task: Multiple choice picture cloze **Pre A1 Starters Speaking Part 3** Task: Answering questions about small pictures	**Pre A1 Starters Reading and Writing Part 2** Task: Writing yes / no answers **Pre A1 Starters Reading and Writing Part 5** Task: Writing one word answers	**Grades 2 and 3** Stating simple facts and answering simple questions
Unit 6	**Pre A1 Starters Listening Part 3** Task: Multiple choice picture cloze **Pre A1 Starters Speaking Part 4** Task: Answering questions to give personal information	**Pre A1 Starters Reading and Writing Part 4** Task: Text cloze **Pre A1 Starters Reading and Writing Part 2** Task: Writing yes / no answers	**Grades 2 and 3** Asking simple questions and giving personal information
Unit 7	**Pre A1 Starters Listening Part 4** Task: Identifying and colouring **Pre A1 Starters Speaking Part 4** Task: Answering questions to give personal information	**Pre A1 Starters Reading and Writing Part 5** Task: Writing one word answers **Pre A1 Starters Reading and Writing Part 3** Task: Spelling words	**Grades 2 and 3** Asking simple questions and giving personal information
Unit 8	**Pre A1 Starters Listening Part 4** Task: Identifying and colouring **Pre A1 Starters Speaking Part 3** Task: Answering questions about small pictures	**Pre A1 Starters Reading and Writing Part 2** Task: Writing yes / no answers **Pre A1 Starters Reading and Writing Part 3** Task: Spelling words	**Grades 2 and 3** Giving and understanding simple instructions
Unit 9	**Pre A1 Starters Listening Part 1** Task: Matching names and children **Pre A1 Starters Speaking Part 4** Task: Answering questions to give personal information	**Pre A1 Starters Reading and Writing Part 5** Task: Writing one word answers **Pre A1 Starters Reading and Writing Part 1** Task: Putting tick / cross answers	**Grades 2 and 3** Stating simple facts and asking and answering simple questions

Macmillan Education
4 Crinan Street
London N1 9XW

A division of Macmillan Education Limited
Companies and representatives throughout the world

Pupil's Book 978-1-380-01357-6
Pupil's Book Pack 978-1-380-01350-7

This edition published 2018

First edition entitled *High Five! English* published 2014 by Macmillan Education Limited

Original series concept design by Tom Cole
Designed by Anthony Godber
Page makeup by emc design ltd
Illustrated by Adrian Barclay, Kathy Baxendale, Leo Broadley, Sam Church, Joelle Dreidemy, Clive Goodyer, Andy Keylock, Andrew Painter, Dusan Pavlic, Ángeles Peinador, Mark Ruffle, Jorge Santillán, Eric Smith, Sholto Walker and Matt Ward.
Cover design by Bigtop Design Limited
Cover photograph by **Getty Images**/iStockphoto Thinkstock Images \ kasto80; Tom Dick and Debbie Productions
Cover illustration by Ángeles Peinador
Course consultants: Rocío Gutiérrez Burgos and Mónica Pérez Is
Picture research by Sally Cole and Fernanda Rocha/ Ikonia LLC
Songs produced and arranged by Tom Dick and Debbie Productions

Authors' acknowledgements
The authors would like to thank everyone at Macmillan who has given help and advice throughout this project. Special thanks from Jo to Carlos, Daniel and Alex for their patience and support during this process. Special thanks from Donna to José, Elisa, Teresa and Marina for their encouragement and enthusiasm.

Acknowledgements
The authors and publishers would like to thank the following teachers for their contribution to the project: Amanda Morrison Prince, Colegio El Parque, La Navata, Madrid; Amaya Carrera García, Colegio Santa Teresa de Jesús, Valladolid; Ana Fernández Sáez, CEIP La Encina, Las Rozas, Madrid; Aránzazu Sánchez Rodríguez, CEIP Rosa Luxemburgo, Madrid; Beatriz García Vaquero, CEIP Mariano José de Larra, Madrid; Carme Tena, Col·legi Sagrada Familia, Tortosa, Tarragona; Cristina Nieto Ruíz de Gaona, CEIP Margarita Salas, Arroyo de la Encomienda, Valladolid; Estíbaliz Medina Martín, CEIP Virgen de Navalazarza, San Agustín de Guadalix, Madrid; Iratxe Zabaleta Zendagorta, Ikastola San Fidel, Guernica, Vizcaya; Lucía Soria García, CEIP Alberto Alcocer, Madrid; M.ª Carmen Lago Muñoz, CEIP Federico García Lorca, Colmenar Viejo, Madrid; Marta Moreno Arroyo, CEIP Vicente Aleixandre, Móstoles, Madrid; Susana Espinel Beneitez, Colegio Grazalema, El Puerto de Santa María, Cádiz; Susana García Pizarro, Ateneu Instructiu, Sant Joan Despi, Barcelona; Virginia Escalona Monreal, CEIP La Encina, Las Rozas, Madrid; Mónica Pérez Is, CEIP Reina Victoria, Madrid; Rocío Gutierrez, CEIP Lepanto, Madrid; Laura Zarzuelo, Colegio Virgen de la Almudena, Collado Villalba, Madrid; Eugenio Domínguez, Colegio Virgen de la Almudena, Collado Villalba, Madrid; Silvia Díez de Rivera, Colegio Orvalle, Las Rozas, Madrid; Maite Crespo, Colegio Jesús Nazareno, Madrid; Silvia Valderrama, CEIP Benito Pérez Galdós, Arganda del Rey, Madrid; Cristina Baeza, CEIP Rosa Chacel, Collado Villalba, Madrid; Leyre Alcalde; CEIP Cortes de Cádiz, Madrid; María Andrés, Colegio Matter Inmaculata, Madrid.

The authors and publishers would like to thank the following for permission to reproduce their photographs:

Alamy Stock Photo/aberCPC p100(sports centre), Alamy Stock Photo/Stephen Dorey ABIPP pp92(sticker), 100(castle), Alamy Stock Photo/Avalon/Photoshot License p68(tr), Alamy/Cultura Creative pp16(cmr), Alamy Stock Photo/Ben Molyneux People p 102(4), Alamy Stock Photo/Chuck Franklin p16(bl), Alamy Stock Photo/Bluefly p66(2), Alamy Stock Photo/Mark Boulton p68(tml), Alamy Stock Photo/ Peter Cripps p11(bl), Alamy Stock Photo/imageBROKER p16(tr), Alamy Stock Photo/Cultura Creative (RF) pp58(mcl, bl), Alamy Stock Photo/Kathy deWitt pp72(sticker), 80(mcl), Alamy Stock Photo/Juice Images p43(br), Alamy Stock Photo/Justin Kase zsixz p90(tl), Alamy Stock Photo/Volodymyr Kaznovskyi p76(camera), Alamy Stock Photo/Yongyut Khasawaong pp28(sticker), 36(tr), Alamy Stock Photo/Terrance Klassen p100(ferris wheel), Alamy Stock Photo/Lasse Kristensen p76(box), Alamy Stock Photo/geogphotos p90(train station), Alamy Stock Photo/Leonid Nyshko p26(tmr), Alamy Stock Photo/Life on white pp36(mcr, br), Alamy Stock Photo/MBI pp96(children), Alamy Stock Photo/Painet Inc. p99(bm), Alamy Stock Photo/Yuri Pancirla p100(factory), Alamy Stock Photo/Malcolm Park p34(inset), Alamy Stock Photo/ONOKY – Photononstop, Alamy Stock Photo/pumkinpie p76(phone), Alamy Stock Photo/James Osmond p48(br), Alamy Stock Photo/Purestock p70(bmr), Alamy Stock Photo/q77photo pp88-89(top banner), Alamy Stock Photo/Radius Images p58(tm), Alamy Stock Photo/Adrian Sherratt p100(safari park), Alamy Stock Photo/Tetra Images p68(ml), Alamy Stock Photo/UpperCut Images p58(br), Alamy Stock Photo/Kevin Wheal p100(circus), Alamy Stock Photo/Phil Wills p90(tr), Alamy Stock Photo/Justin Kase zninez p80(mc); **BananaStock** p102(5); **BrandX** pp76(clock), 80(tcl); **Comstock** pp18(sticker), 26(bml, tl); **Corbis** pp32(teeth), 40(sticker), 48(tmr, bl), 80(mr); **Creatas** p35(mr); **Fancy** p68(mcl); **Fotolibra**/Kristensen Lasse p76(watch); **Getty Images** pp26(tm, bm, tr), 32(face, tail), 36(mr, bl, tm, bm, mcl), Getty Images/Blend Images/Inti St Clair p16(mcl), Getty Images/Blend Images/KidStock p31(br), Getty Images/Brand X Pictures/ moodboard p80(mcr), Getty Images/ChristopherBernard p58(ml), Getty Images/Corbis documentary/Pawel Libera pp90(museum), 91(museum), Getty Images/Corbis/Helen King pp82(sticker), 90(bakery), Getty Images/Corbis/Mango Productions p70(mr), Getty Images/ Corbis/VCG p99(mc), Getty Images/Cultura/Monty Rakusen p105(tr), Getty Images/ Creatas Video+/aaom50 p91(ml), Getty Images/Creatas Video+/helivideo p59(mr), Getty Images/Creatas Video/kali9 p17(mr), Getty Images/Creatas Video/MediaJB p37(mcr), Getty Images/Creatas Video+/NordicMoonlight p59(ml), Getty Images/Creatas Video+/ Simon Podgorsek p49(ml), Getty Images/Creatas Video+/sergey02 p101(mr), Getty Images/ Creatas Video/SimonSkafar p69(mr), Getty Images/Creatas Video/SolStock pp17(ml, mcr), 49(mr), Getty Images/Creatas Video+/UtlanovD p59(mcl), Getty Images/Creatas Video+/ Wavebreakmedia p101(ml), Getty Images/Nick David p95(br), Getty Images/DigitalVision p99(br), Getty Images/DigitalVision/Sonya Farrell p69(mcl), Getty Images/DigitalVision/ PeopleImages p16(mr), Getty Images/Dorling Kindersley/Steve Gorton p11(box), Getty Images/Dorling Kindersley/Cyril Laubscher p32(winds), Getty Images/Dorling Kindersley/ Tim Ridley pp78-79(top banner), Getty Images/E+/jimkruger p105(mc), Getty Images/ E+/Imgorthand p101(mcl), Getty Images/E+/ollo p24(top banner), Getty Images/E+/ SolStock p17(mcl), Getty Images/E+/vpopovic pp106-115(top banner), 117(top banner), Getty Images/Glow Decor p80(tcr), Getty Images/Monalyn Gracia/Corbis p16(tm), Getty Images/Hero Images p68(br), Getty Images/Image Bank Film/The Time Lapse Company p27(mr), Getty Images/Image Bank Film/Deluxe Photo p37(mcr), Getty Images/Image Bank Film: Signature/Ariel Skelley p69(ml), Getty Images/Images Bazaar p101(mcr), Getty Images/Image Source p16(bc), 75(br), Getty Images/iStock/Getty Images Plus/Madllen p26(tmr), Getty Images/iStock/margouillatphotos p27(mcl), Getty Images/iStock/Vjom pp66-67(top banner), Getty Images/iStock Unreleased/LPETTET p90(bc), Getty Images/ ITN pp37(ml), 91(mcl, mr), Getty Images/Juice Images/Ian Lishman p63(br), Getty Images/ Jeffoto pp98-99(top banner), Getty Images/mgkayathis p76(radio), Getty Images/Mint Images p105(br), Getty Images/Moment Video RF p27(ml), Getty Images/Nature Picture Library p34(4), Getty Images/Greg Newton/ArcaidImages p80(tr), Getty Images/Oxford Scientific/Les Stocker p34(2), Getty Images/Photodisc/Digital Vision p70(mcr), Getty Images/Photodisc/Andrew Dernie p35(ml, mc), Getty Images/Photographer's Choice/Nancy Brown p99(bl), Getty Images/Photographer's Choice/Peter Dazeley p70(ml), Getty Images/ Photographer's Choice RF/Pando Hall p 96(men), Getty Images/Photolibrary/Susan Barr p102(6), Getty Images/Photolibrary/Les Stocker p104(4), Getty Images/PickStock p11(boy), Getty Images/PJB/Photographer's Choice p34(top banner), Getty Images/Jaskunwar Singh/ EyeEm pp14-15(top banner), Getty Images/Stockbyte/George Doyle p21(br), Getty Images/ StockFood p68(mcr), Getty Images/Stone/Jodie Griggs p104(3), Getty Images/Stone/ Bob Thomas p100(aquarium), Getty Images/Tetra Images p102(3), Getty Images/The Image Bank/Jae Rew p102(2), Getty Images/Verve/Fluorescent Films Ltd p37(mcl), Getty Images/Vetta/GlobalStock p85(br), Getty Images/Vetta/simonkr p49(mcr), Getty Images/ Vetta/RichVintage p104(bm), Getty Images/VisitBritain/Pawel Libera p104(tr); **Image Source** pp48(bml), 50(sticker), 58(mr), 96(women), Image Source/Allen and Kleantho p70(mcl), Image Source/Charles Gullung CM p48(tr); **John Foxx Images** pp32(body, beak), 36(ml); **Macmillan Publishers Ltd.** /Paul Bricknell p80(ml), Macmillan Publishers Ltd./Lisa Payne p11(tr, tl); **PhotoAlto** p26(br); **Photodisc** p36(tl), PhotoDisc/Getty Images p48(tml); **Plainpicture**/Design Pics p48(bmr), Plainpicture/Johner/Roine Magnusson p46-47(top banner); **REX**/Shutterstock/David Bagnall p105(tl); **Stockbyte** pp16(ml), 48(bm); **Shutterstock**/adriaticfoto p90(ml), Shutterstock/BCFC p81(ml), Shutterstock/ PERLA BERANT WILDER p27(mcr), Shutterstock/ber1a pp56-57, Shutterstock/Caftor p69(mcr), Shutterstock/Nadya Eugene p68(tmr), Shutterstock/futureGalore p90(mcl), Shutterstock/ JIANG HONGYAN p26(bl), Shutterstock/humbak p104(5), Shutterstock/jan kranendonk p104(tl), Shutterstock/Len44ik p16(tl), Shutterstock/elena moiseeva p105(mr), Shutterstock/ Most popular p49(mcl), Shutterstock/OnlyFOOD p25(sandwich), Shutterstock/ppart p104(1), Shutterstock/Sasa Prudkov p105(tm), Shutterstock/Taiga p105(bc), Shutterstock/ Tomsickova Tatyana p59(mcr), Shutterstock/Max Topchii p104(bl), Shutterstock/Alastair Wallace p81(mcl); **SuperStock**/Jeff Greenberg/age fotostock p100(water park), SuperStock/ Stock Connection p100(theatre), SuperStock/Jochen Tack/imageBROKER p90(post office), SuperStock/View Pictures Ltd p90(fire station); **123RF**/paffy p104(br), 123RF/Angela Waye p104(2).

Photographs re-used on stickers:
Alamy Stock Photo; BrandX; Comstock Images; Corbis; Fancy; Getty Images; Image Source; John Foxx Images; Macmillan Publishers Ltd.; PhotoAlto; Photodisc; Plainpicture; Shutterstock; Stockbyte; SuperStock.

Commissioned photographs by Lisa Payne pp6, 12, 13, 14, 16(b), 22, 23, 24, 25(l), 32(b), 33(b), 34(tr, cl, bl), 44(b), 45(b), 46, 48(b), 53(br), 54(b), 55(b), 56, 58(b), 64(b), 65(b), 66(1, 3, 4, tr, tm), 71, 76(b), 77(b), 78, 86(b), 87(b), 88, 90(b), 96(b), 97(b), 98, 100(b), 102(tr, tl), 103, 104(tr), 105(b), 106(b), 107(b), 108(b), 109(b), 110(b), 111(b), 112(b), 113(b), 114(b) and Tom Dick and Debbie Productions pp17(t, b), 27(t, b), 37(t, b), 49(t, b), 59(t,b), 69(t, b), 81(t, b), 91(t, b), 97(b), 101(t, b).

Printed and bound in Uruguay

2022
48

Unit 1

Unit 2

Unit 3

Unit 4

Unit 5

Unit 6

Unit 7

Unit 8

Unit 9